THE JEWS AND ISRAEL
PAST, PRESENT, AND FUTURE
IN ROMANS 9, 10, AND 11

By

Charles J. Kriessman III, Ph. D.

Disclaimer

The author of this work has quoted the writers of many articles and books. This does not mean that the author endorses or recommends the works of others. If the author quotes someone, it does not mean that he agrees with all of the author's tenets, statements, concepts, or words, whether in the work quoted or any other work of the author. There has been no attempt to alter the meaning of the quotes; and therefore, some of the quotes are long in order to give the entire sense of the passage.

Copyright © 2015 by Dr. Charles J. Kriessman
All Rights Reserved
Printed in the United States of America

REL006201: Religion: Biblical Studies - Topical

ISBN: 978-0-9962591-3-2

All Scripture quotes are from the King James Bible except those verses compared and then the source is identified.

No part of this work may be reproduced without the expressed consent of the publisher, except for brief quotes, whether by electronic, photocopying, recording, or information storage and retrieval systems.

Address All Inquiries To:
THE OLD PATHS PUBLICATIONS, Inc.
142 Gold Flume Way
Cleveland, Georgia, U.S.A.

Web: www.theoldpathspublications.com
E-mail: TOP@theoldpathspublications.com

1.0

DEDICATION

This book is dedicated to all believers who are truly saved and serve the Lord. It is hoped that they would understand and support Jews and Israel and spread the Gospel to them without fear. Also it is important that Christians not contribute to the Christian Anti-Semitism sentiment prevalent among Jews but help restore friendly relations between the two groups.

To Jews it is hoped that you realize who your Redeemer is before it is too late.

To Messianic Jews, since you know who your messiah is, that you serve Him in the faith once delivered to the saints. There is no need for any observances of the feast, the law, or any of the Hebrew Roots Movements.

To unsaved Gentiles, that you would have an understanding and compassion for Jews and come to a saving grace of the Lord Jesus Christ.

Furthermore, thanks to Dr. and Mrs. Williams for their tireless work to complete these pages and turn them into a book. May God bless them for their Godly counsel.

TABLE OF CONTENTS

DEDICATION 3
TABLE OF CONTENTS 5
SOME TERMS 9
INTRODUCTION 21
    "Israel Cannot Exist"................................... 23
    The Miracle of Israel 26
    Other Menaces... 30
    Holocaust Deniers 31
    Willis A. Carto... 36
    Harry Elmer Barnes 39
    Islamic Negationism 44
    Shylock.. 46
    Consequences... 52
    Support for Israel...................................... 53
    A Warning 56
    Conversion of Jews.................................... 60
    Be A Witness to the Jews 63
    The Purpose 65
CHAPTER 1: A History of Ancient Israel 67
    To Make a Nation 68
    God's Call To Abraham.............................. 69
    The Abrahamic Covenant........................... 69
    ISAAC... 75
    Moses 91
    The Call of Moses 93
    The Freeing of Israel............................... 104
    The Institution of the Passover................ 106
    The Spiritual Side of Passover.................. 110
    Death of Firstborn 113
    Deliverance 114
    Abrahamic Covenant Revisited 117
    Unconditional or Conditional Covenants....... 121
    Conditional Covenants 122
    Unconditional Covenants 123
    Mosaic Covenant 124

The Components of the Law	132
The Law Fulfilled	135
Christ Fulfilled the Law	137
The Tabernacle	139
Physical Description of the Tabernacle	141
Christ in the Furniture of the Tabernacle	145
The Brazen Altar	145
The Brazen Laver	148
The Table of Shewbread	150
The Golden Candlestick	151
The Golden Altar of Incense	153
The Veil	156
The Ark of the Covenant	158
The Mercy Seat	161
CHAPTER 2: Romans 9	**165**
Introduction	165
A Theodicy	167
Paul and Romans 9	171
Romans 9	172
Paul Deeply Sorrowful. Vs. 1-3	172
Physical Israelites Vs. 4,5	175
Israel Identified. Vs. 6-13	176
God's Choice. Vs. 1-18	180
Quit finding Fault. Vs. 19-24	183
Rejection of Israel Vs. 25-29	186
Reality and Reason. Vs. 30-33.	189
CHAPTER 3: Romans 10	**193**
Introduction	193
Lost State Vs. 1-4	193
No Difference Vs. 5-12	196
Whosoever Vs. 13-15	202
Israel Rejects Gospel Vs. 16,17	204
The Message Changes Course Vs. 18-21	205
Chapter 4: Romans 11	**209**
I, Paul: Vs. 1	209
The Saved remnant Vs. 2-6	211
Israel is Blind Vs. 7-10	215
God's Purposes Declared Vs. 11-12	219

TABLE OF CONTENTS

Purposes of God Proven Vs. 13-15 222
Principle of Israel's Restoration Vs. 16-22 .. 224
Possible Restoration Vs. 23-24 232
The Promise of Restoration Vs. 25-29 234
The Mercies of God Vs. 30-32 242
Paul's Response to God's Ways Vs. 33-36 244
CHAPTER 5: Supersessionism and Antisemitism 249
 Introduction 249
 Definition 250
 Replacement... 252
 Positions of Supersessionists 254
 Premises 255
 Non-Literal Fulfillment? 257
 Romans 11:26 259
 Antisemitism... 262
 What is Anti-Semitism? 263
 Attitudes 265
 Martin Luther 267
 The Protocols 270
 Its Influence 271
ENDNOTES 275
 Introduction 275
 CHAPTER 1 276
 CHAPTER 2 277
 CHAPTER 3 277
 CHAPTER 4 277
 CHAPTER 5 277
BIBLIOGRAPHY 279
 Books 279
 ARTICLES 282
INDEX OF WORDS AND PHRASES 285
ABOUT THE AUTHOR 293

SOME TERMS

Abomination of Desolation – A future event taking place in the middle of the Tribulation or fourty-two months after Antichrist signs a peace treaty with Israel. The daily sacrifice in the Temple will be replaced with a speaking image of Antichrist which will be commanded to be worshipped as their Saviour.

Abrahamic Covenant – An eternal, unconditional set of promises given by God to Abraham in Genesis 12:1-3.

Allah – The religion of Allah's central deity goes by the name, "Allah." The Muslims claim that Allah is a continuity of the Christian God. Allah is a pre-Islamic name which has been shown to correspond to the Babylonian BEL, (Hastings, 1908). The moon god Allah was married to the sun goddess. Mohammed was raised in the moon-god Allah cult and took Allah to be the only true god of Islam.

Amillennialism – The Millennial view which says that the 1000 years in Revelation 20 is symbolic and not literal. Denies a literal 1000 year reign of Jesus Christ and attributes the binding of Satan, the resurrection, and the earthly reign of Christ as symbols of this church age and not of the future.

Antichrist – Future leader of the world who makes a peace agreement with Israel then breaks it 3-1/2 years into the Tribulation. Meets his end when he is defeated at the Battle of Armageddon by the Lord Jesus Christ when he and the false prophet are both cast into the Lake of Fire.

Antisemitism – Hatred for the Jewish people. Grew out of ancient Jews and on-Jewish neighbors developing and leading separate social and religious lives. This led to intolerance and suspicion resulting from these differences which has led to fear and hatred.

Apostasy – From "apostasia" meaning to fall away from. It is a deliberate and complete abandonment of the faith once delivered to the Saints. (Jude 3).

Atavism – Recurrence, throwback.

SOME TERMS

Backsliding – This term is used by God in the Old Testament to denote Israel's spiritual condition. (Jeremiah 3:6)

Biblical Literacy – A condition wherein a person has enough knowledge of basic, fundamental Bible facts and principles that he/she can make competent judgments about and make intelligent conclusions as to what God has revealed to man.

Blasphemy – Word used to show defamation and speaking evil of someone. The range of use spans from taking the Lord's name in vain to Pharaoh's charging the Lord as being evil.

Church – Those saved between the day of Pentecost (Acts 2) and the Rapture. Includes saved Jews and saved Gentiles. Those Saints from before Pentecost and after the Rapture are not part of the church. There are distinctions between groups of Saints in history; Old Testament Saints, Church Saints, Tribulation saints, and Millennial Saints.

Covenant – A solemn agreement between groups or individuals. God made Covenants with Israel as well as Abraham, Adam, Noe, Moses, and David. Usually divided into conditional and unconditional covenants.

Covenant Theology – Based on the theology of John Calvin and developed by Johannes Cocceius. Has two main points; the Covenant of Works and the Covenant of Grace. Thus the relationship between God and man, according to this theology is governed by agreements.

Davidic Covenant – Found in 2 Samuel 7:12-17. This Covenant reaffirms and extends God's Covenant with Abraham. It is unconditional and along with the Abrahamic Covenant makes up the basis for Israel's future existence, restoration, and the Kingdom.

Diaspora – The word means to scatter. The Diaspora of the Jews came in 70 A.D. with the destruction of the Temple and Jerusalem. The Jews were cast out of their land and scattered throughout the Nations for 1900 years. The Nation of Israel in the modern, latter days was reborn in 1948.

SOME TERMS

Dispensation(s) – Divisions of human history into periods of time whereby God has made himself known, and continues to make himself known, revealing his eternal program and purposes as pertaining to men upon the earth. Knowledge of God's intents enables one to know how to read and rightly divide the words of God.

Eisegesis – The incorrect way to interpret Scripture whereby the interpreter reads into the words of God meaning that is not there. The correct method of Biblical interpretation is called exegesis.

Eschatology – From the Greek "eschatos" meaning last things. It is the teaching of future events or last things. God's dealings with Israel, the Church, the Nations, death, resurrection, judgment, and the afterlife, are all included. End time events center around the books of Revelation and Daniel which contain the greatest amount of prophecy relating to latter day events.

Futurism – The orthodox view of Eschatology. This is literal interpretation of literal events spanning the as-yet-to-be-fulfilled events of Revelation six thru twenty, and corresponding to the 10th week of Daniel.

Gentiles – From the Greek "Ethos" meaning heathen. The Jews see Gentiles as being non-Jewish. For someone born-again, one who is neither Jewish nor Christian.

Intercalation – An insertion of a period of time in a calendar.

Islam – Monotheistic religion adhering to the Qur'an, considered by Muslims to be the Word of God. Also based on the teachings and writing of Mohammed, considered by them to be the last prophet of God.

Jihad – A noun which means struggle in Arabic. Westerners understand the word to mean "holy war" and in one sense of the word it is an action to protect the faith, which is understood to be the teachings of Mohammed. Proponents swear that Jihad is not a violent concept.

Judaism – The religion and culture of the Jews. Modern Judaism is based on the Torah, on belief that God is one, spiritual and eternal.

The Jews are especially called by God, and that their land can be traced back to Abraham. They still look for the coming of the Messiah, and observe the Sabbath on Saturday. Judaism is a Christ-rejecting, Christ-hating religion.

Messiah – Transliterated from the Hebrew word "Mesiha," meaning to anoint. The root meaning is understood as "the anointed of God," or "King." "Christ" is the Greek equivalent of the Hebrew "Messiah." In the New Testament Jesus Christ is the Messiah, testified by Peter than anointed Jesus, "with the Holy ghost and with power." (Acts 10:38). Jesus Christ is the promised King who will appear in th eend time to rule during the Millennium.

Monotheism – Believing that there is only one member of the Triune God. This is the Judaistic belief of the Hebrew people.

Mosaic Covenant – A conditional Covenant God made with Israel. God gave Israel the law as its constitution and the nation had to obey God's laws to stay in the land and enjoy the blessing of God. In this Covenant God promised to make Israel "a kingdom of priests and a holy nation." (Exodus 19:6). The New Covenant replaces this Covenant and fulfills the promises made in Jeremiah 31:31-34 and quoted in Hebrews 8.

Mosaic Law – Refers to the law given by God to Moses on Mount Sinai for the Jewish people. It included the best known of the laws, the Ten Commandments. The law of Moses also contained all the civil and ceremonial law, which numbers more than six hundred and thirty.

Mystery – In the bible something unknown and under the circumstances beyond knowing. Truth once hidden can now be revealed by special revelation.

New Covenant – (Luke 22:20; 1 Cor 11:25; 2 Cor 3:6; Heb 8:8; 8:13; 9:15; 12:24.

The New Covenant in God's promise of blessing to men through the Lord Jesus Christ. Christians share the spiritual parts of the New Covenant through Christ Jesus. To Israel, God promises to eternally restore them to their land and renew their hears to obey Him. (Jer. 31:31). It replaces the Mosaic Covenant.

Parenthesis – An interlude or interval, an intervening or interruptive period. For example: a distinct interlude in God's program for Israel clearly appears in the prophecy of Daniel's 70 weeks. Daniel 9:24-27.

Parousia – In the Greek it means, "A being present." Refers to the second coming of Christ.

Palestinian Covenant – An eternal, unconditional covenant that reaffirms Israel's title deed to the land. Israel will be cast out of the land for their disobedience; there is a future repentance of Israel; the Messiah returns and restores Israel to its land and will receive her full blessing.

Postmillennialism – In the theology of the last things, says that Christ returns after the Millennium, the thousand year period following the Tribulation. Says that the Church will build the World according to Biblical foundations and at the end of the thousand years Christ will come to reign over a Christianized World.

Premillennialism – According to Revelation 20:4 Christ will return to Earth before the Millennium to begin his 1000 year earthly kingdom. In the literal interpretation of the Scriptures the Church is raptured before the Tribulation and the Saints return with

Christ at his second coming and reign with him for the 1000 year Millennium.

Quran – The central text of Islam which Muslims believe to be the direct revelation from God. Muslims believe the words of the Quran were revealed to Mohammed through the Angel Gabriel over a period of 23 years.

Renascent – Rising again into being.

Replacement Theology –
Supersessionism says that God is through with Israel along with the promises and blessings God made to them. These are now fulfilled in the Church which is the New Israel. Besides the Roman Catholic Church, a number of Protestants and modern day Christians hold to supersessionist views.

Saint – A born-again, Bible believing Christian.

Second Coming – Jesus Christ told his Disciples that he would go away and come back, again to gather his own. (John 14:3). For dispensationalists it will be two-phase event. Jesus Christ will come in the air (1 Thessalonians 4:16) in a pre-tribulation rapture in the first phase. Then at the end of the Seven Year Tribulation Jesus will return with his Saints to the Earth and establish the Millennium Kingdom (Revelation 20: 11-15).

Sharia Law – The sacred law of Islam. Based on the Koran, it involves both civil and criminal justice as well as regulating individual conduct, both person and moral. As applied in the approximately 50 Islamic states, there are multiple layers of doctrine based on original religious Mohammedan texts resulting in a multitude of different interpretations and different legal results.

Son of Man – All descendants of Adam are the sons of man (Isaiah 51:12). However, the title "Son of Man" belongs only to Jesus Christ. Found in some 78 places in the Gospels, Jesus used this expression for himself to show his compassion and love for all mankind. The two natures of Christ, as both man and God is called 'hypostatic union."

Theophany – Also known as a "Christophamy" is the manifestation in some visual, physical form of the pre-incarnate Christ. Even though Judaism rejects the doctrine of the Trinity, the truth is that theophonies in the Old testament, using other terms, are actually the manifestation of the second person of the God head.

Theology – From the Greek words, "theos" meaning God, and "logos" meaning discourse or study, theology is the study of God. This is accomplished through a systematic study of the doctrine of God, his proof of existence, knowability, person, attributes, names, works, decree and government. Also included is the Doctrine of the Trinity.

Vituperative – Uttering or given to censure: containing or characterized by verbal abuse. Bitter railing, condemnation.

Zionism – The movement devoted to re-establishing the Jewish people back to their land of Israel. It found fulfillment in a Jewish State on May 14, 1948 when the British ended their rule and the State of Israel was recognized. Today, "Christian Zionism" take a premillennial stance in its active support of Israel.

All or some parts of the definitions of these terms were culled from: "Theologicalisms," Randy Smith; "The Compact Dictionary of Doctrinal Words," Terry L. Miethe; and "Way of Life Encyclopedia of the Bible." David Cloud.

INTRODUCTION

It is surprising the number of writers out there who blame everything that has happened to the Jews on God's Holy Scriptures. The deep seated war on the Jew is also blamed for its perpetuation on the Christian churches. It is referred to as: "Cold hate preached in the Christian churches, seminars, and Sunday schools. The clergymen do not tell you whom to kill; they just tell you whom to hate."[1]

We as Americans need to foster an understanding of Israel and its people and to add a voice to responsible moral and political decisions respecting Israel and its place in the Middle East. We need to understand how Israel came to be and its relationship with God from Abrahamic times to the present. It follows that the future of Israel has a foundation in God's words and will extend to the end of time and beyond. Much controversy arises when history, past, present, and future collides with multicultural religious thought.

The multitude of prophesies yet to come about concerning the nation of Israel should give pause to those who believe that God has abandoned Israel.

> *"Behold, I will make Jerusalem a cup of trembling unto all the people round*

> about, when they shall be in the siege against Judah and against Jerusalem.
>
> And in that day will I make Jerusalem a burdensome stone for all people: all that burden themselves with it shall be cut in pieces, though all the people of the Earth be gathered together against it." (Zechariah 12:2.3)

All of Israel's neighbors, who are enemies, are united in opposition to Israel. It is the religion of Islam that unites Israel's enemies against her and it is their stated unequivocal goal to destroy all the Jews. Israel is the main topic of our King James Bible.

There have been more than enough prophesies already fulfilled in the long history of Israel to prove that the God of Israel is the true God.

> "Come, and let us return unto the Lord: for he hath torn, and he will heal us; he hath smitten, and he will bind us up.
>
> After two days will he revive us: in the third day he will raise us up, and we shall live in his sight." (Hosea 6:1,2)

This section of scripture from Hosea was being spoken to post-exilic Jews from Babylon. God was predicting what was to come to pass in the latter days. Some two thousand years, two days, from this prophecy Israel once again took their place in the family of nations on May 14, 1948.

INTRODUCTION

"Israel Cannot Exist"

> *"For I am with thee, saith the LORD, to save thee: though I make a full end of all nations whither I have scattered three, yet will I not make a full end of thee:"* (Jeremiah 30:11)

Israel's enemies of Fatah, the PLO, and Hezbollah have in their founding documents declarations of their mission to destroy Israel. Their clear and present danger is directly aimed at the nation of Israel, but their evil goals also endanger the human rights and democratic values of the Western world as a whole.

Peace for Israel will not come until their Messiah, the Lord Jesus Christ, comes to them at the end of the Tribulation. Hamas, the terrorist organization, has views in their charter that are both racist and genocidal. These are the people that represent the Palestinian people who want their own terrorist state. The Hamas Covenant: In the name of the most merciful Allah; "Israel will exist and will continue to exist until Islam will obliterate it, just as it obliterated others before it."[2]

> The Islamic Resistance Movement does not believe that the land of Israel is rightfully the Jews' property. Article eleven of the Hamas Charter states:
>
> The Islamic Resistance Movement

23

> believes that the land of Palestine is an Islamic Waqf consecrated for future Moslem generations until Judgement Day. It, or any part of it, should not be squandered: it, or any part of it, should not be given up. Neither a single Arab country nor all Arab countries, neither any king or president, nor all the kings and presidents, neither any organization nor all of them, be they Palestinian or Arab, possess the right to do that. Palestine is an Islamic Waqf consecrated for Moslem generations until Judgement Day.[3]

These terrorists will have nothing to do with the Bible's proclamation of the land given by God to the Jews through Abraham in perpetuity. This is a denial of God and His words. In their minds the Land of Palestine is in control of the Arabs and Sharia Law. The West, and especially the United States, could save a lot of time and energy by reading what these terrorists believe in negotiating. Article Thirteen of the Hamas Charter states:

> Initiatives, and so-called peaceful solutions and international conferences, are in contradiction to the principles of the Islamic Resistance Movement. [4]

Israel knows this and will not sit down with these terrorists until they change their Charter. The United States must change their direction in trying to force Israel into something that they know is wrong. The

INTRODUCTION

United States must stop taking an anti-Israel position and being pro-terrorist.

Article 13 of the Hamas Charter continues:

> There is no solution for the Palestinian question except through Jihad. Initiatives, proposals and international conferences are all a waste of time and vain endeavors.

The Islamic Waqf refers to an inalienable religious endowment in Sharia Law in which a voluntary and irrevocable dedication of wealth or land is used for Muslim religious or charitable purposes. A good example of such an arrangement is the Jerusalem Islamic Waqf. The present Waqf controls and manages the currently built Islamic edifices around and including the Al-Aqsa Mosque in the Temple Mount in Old Jerusalem. The Waqf has had governess over that region since the Muslim re-conquest of the Kingdom of Jerusalem in 1187. The Waqf consists of the director, the Grand Mufti of Jerusalem, and the Islamic Council. After Israel captured Old Jerusalem as a result of the Six-Day War of June 1967, Israel allowed the Waqf possession of the Temple Mount up to this day.

The problem is, just as the Islamist will not relinquish the Islamic Waqf in Jerusalem, they still consider all of the present day Land of Israel as their consecrated Islamic Waqf never to be given up. They are instilling in the minds of their Moslem generations that the Palestinian problem is a religious problem and it will be waged on that basis. This is the basis upon the notion that Israel cannot exist. Article Twenty-seven of the Hamas Charter:

> ...we are unable to exchange the present or future Islamic Palestine with the secular idea. The Islamic nature of Palestine is part of our religion and whoever takes his religion lightly is a loser.

This is their Replacement of Israel theology. No one can question their resoluteness or determinism in their pursuit. Their devotion to their cause and to their God is absolute. Article Eight of the Hamas Charter states this martyrdom complex:

> Allah is its target, the Prophet is its model, the Koran its Constitution: Jihad is its path and death for the sake of Allah is the loftiest of its wishes.

The reality of the threat to destroy Israel faces her every day. Israel is hated by the nations of the world because it was a divinely formed nation of priests and kings to all the World.

The Miracle of Israel

Ever since God called Abraham in order to form Israel as a nation unto himself, Satan has tried endlessly to eradicate the Jews from the face of the earth. The very fact that the Jewish

INTRODUCTION

people have survived from the Exodus from Egypt to this present day is nothing short of miraculous.

The President of Israel, Ezer Weizmann, said in 1996,

> "We have dreamed towers of yearning, of Jerusalem, result, of Jerusalem united, of a peace that will swiftly and speedily establish us in our days. Amen."[5]

Jerusalem means City of Peace, but it is the most violent city of Earth. Jerusalem itself has been besieged, captured, or completely destroyed forty-six times, beginning with King David.[6]

This is the result of the battle between God and the Devil being centered in Jerusalem. Satan wants to destroy Jerusalem, the Jews, and Israel in order to prevent the Lord Jesus Christ form appearing on His holy hill of Zion to bring in His Kingdom. By looking at all the events of history, from the dispersion, to the Holocaust, and since 1947, should convince most people of a higher power directing the destiny of the tiny nation of Israel so that they have survived until now.

This history of Israel and how they have survived relentless Satanic attacks will be addressed in later chapters. So, when we study the history (survival) of the Jewish people through time, we see it is nothing short of miraculous. The whole credit for Jewish survival through the years has to be laid at the foot of God.

> *"For thou hast confirmed to thyself thy people Israel to be a people unto thee forever; and thou, LORD, art become their God."* (2 Samuel 7:24)

God and the people of Israel are unequivocally linked together, and will be forever.

> *"Thus saith the LORD, which giveth the sun for a light by day, and the ordinances of the moon and of the stars for a light by night... If those ordinances depart from before me, saith the LORD, then the seed of Israel also shall cease from being a nation before me forever."* (Jeremiah 31:35, 36)

Incredibly God is saying that the whole universe serves as the visual evidence for the eternal preservation of the nation of Israel. The words of God state that if the sun, the moon, and the stars are somehow destroyed, then the nation of Israel would be destroyed.

Jews today, who know any of their own history and the Old Testament, do believe that continuing to survive as a nation is a miracle. To Jews this can be the only realistic explanation. David Ben Gurion, the first Prime

INTRODUCTION

Minister of Israel, said: "A Jew who does not believe in miracles is not a realist."

King Louis XIV of France asked Blaise Pascal, the great French philosopher, to give him proof of God. Pascal answered: "Why, the Jews, your Majesty – the Jews."[7]

Pascal knew that the fact that the Jewish people survived until the time he was alive was nothing short of a supernatural phenomenon. Here was a famous world philosopher and he had no logical explanation for the survival of the Jew other than it was a miracle. Many other famous people could not explain it. Mark Twain, who was an agnostic wrote:

> "The Egyptian, the Babylonian, and the Persian rose, filled the planet with sound and splendor, then passed away. The Greek and Roman followed, and they are gone. All things are mortal, but the Jew. All other forces pass, but he remains. What is the secret to his immortality?"[8]

Not only by His promise has God kept Israel, Satan's attempts at destroying Israel, thereby destroying the seed line of the promised Messiah, has been thwarted. Many times Satan has tried to nullify God's promise of a seed line for Messiah, and every time God has intervened supernaturally. No other people on earth has suffered as have the Jews. Satan has attempted throughout their history to wipe out the Jews.

Briefly, this persecution began with Pharaoh in Egypt who attempted to attack Israel as they crossed the Red Sea. The Assyrians in 721 B.C. slaughtered many Jews and took the northern ten tribes into captivity. Then followed Nebuchadnezzar in 586 B.C. Jews suffered from the Greeks and the Romans who were responsible for their dispersal into the nations. The Middle Ages brought much persecution against them. Satan then used Hitler to murder six million Jewish people. Up to this point in time the Devil has failed to do away with the Jews and the nation of Israel.

Other Menaces

Satan is not done. Besides hostile neighbors, other sinister attacks from the pit of Hell include Anti-Semitism and Replacement Theology. These will be addressed in depth later also. Anti-Semitism sprang from an unlikely source; the early Church, which included some but not all of the Church fathers, on through the Roman Catholic Church, and re-emerging through Martin Luther. Anti-Semitism is rearing its ugly head in Europe and is spreading into Canada and the United states.

We will focus on such virulent anti-Jew material as "The Protocols of the Elders" which forms the basis of 20th Century Anti-Semitism.

This fraudulent document must be denounced in no uncertain terms. It supposedly contains an account of a Jewish plan to dominate the world. This has fueled the flames of imaginary Jewish global conspiracies, which have spawned, incredibly, contained in the Hamas Charter. Globally an over-representation of Jewish people on control of government, the media, academia, and financial institutions will be couched in terms of a Jewish Lobby."[9]

Holocaust Deniers

Another threatening menace is today's Holocaust deniers. The Anti-Defamation League says that only 54 percent of the world's population has even heard of the Holocaust. The Holocaust is that horrendous act during World War II, roughly from 1940 to 1945, where Adolph Hitler gassed and burned up to six million European Jews.

Only one-third of the world's people believe that the events of the Holocaust are historically accurate as described in historical accounts. Lots of people say that the number of Jews killed by the Nazis is exaggerated and lots of people say that it is a myth. It has been 70 years since the closing of the Auschwitz Concentration Camp, and all of the concentration camps, and yet two-thirds of the world's population, do not know how the

Holocaust happened or the just outright deny it.

According to the Anti-Defamation League less than 15% of all Africans had heard about the Holocaust and had the highest percentage of those who doubt it even happened. Those in Asia followed with about 25%. Over half of the Middle Easterners and a third of Africans and Asians believe that the numbers of Jews killed has been distorted over time. [10]

When considering belief or denial among religious groups, it is found that Hindus and Muslims were more likely to believe that the number of Holocaust deaths, were exaggerated.

Christian groups, Buddhists, and those with no religious affiliation trailed the top two groups (Hindus and Muslims) by a wide margin in believing the Holocaust number have been exaggerated. One thing is clear, the more time goes on the fainter the memory of the Jewish genocide of the Holocaust becomes. This is dangerous for the nation of Israel and for the rest of the world, for the same atrocities could repeat themselves. What is also frightening is that 75% of the global population get their information about Jews and the Holocaust from television, the Internet, and newspapers.

INTRODUCTION

Holocaust denial can be described as denying the genocide of six million Jews by Hitler and the Nazis during World War II. They can believe that the Nazi government had no policy in place to exterminate Jews, that the death camps did not use gas chambers to murder Jews, and that the number of Jews that died during World War II was only a fraction of the number advertised. Holocaust deniers do not like the term denial to describe what they consider legitimate revision of history. They ignore the overwhelming historical facts and base their opinionated results on predetermined conclusions dreamed up in the recesses of their minds. To them it is all a Jewish conspiracy to further the interests of Jews at the expense of all others. For all these reasons, and more, Holocaust denial can be considered the most hideous form of Anti-Semitism on the planet. The denial type of historical interpretation should never be confused with legitimate historical revisionism, which concerns itself with historical events' causes and consequences generally.

Sometimes referred to as "negationism," from the French term "negationnisme" introduced by Henry Rousso, Holocaust deniers attempt to re-write history by minimizing, denying, or simply ignoring essential facts."[11]

Negationism means the denial of historical crimes against humanity. It is not a re-interpretation of known facts, but the denial of known facts. The term negationism has gained currency as the name of a movement to deny a specific crimes against humanity, the Nazi genocide on the Jews in 1941-1945, also known as the Holocaust (Greek: complete burning) of the "shoah" (Hebrew: disaster). Negationism is mostly identified with the effort at re-writing history in such a way that the fact of the Holocaust is omitted. [12]

It is very perilous to just skip over such a world changing, horrific event such as the Holocaust and pretend that it never occurred. Just the concealment of the fact from millions and millions of people even knowing must never happen. Yet there are thousands of deniers who are given a stage and a platform to spew forth their venom. Two of these influential deniers will be spotlighted here in some detail, with a partial list of deniers to follow.

Austin App (1902-1984) taught Medieval English Literature at Scranton University and LaSalle University. During World War II, App was sympathetic to and defended Germans and the Nazis. He is considered the first major American Holocaust denier. [13]

INTRODUCTION

Mr. App wrote articles for the Anti-Semitic magazine "Common Sense." All of App's writings, his books, writing for magazines and newspapers, inspired the Institute for Historical Review, founded in 1978 in California and exists only for the denial of the Holocaust.

In 1973 App published eight "incontrovertible (indisputable) assertions "about the Holocaust. These appeared in his 1973 pamphlet "The Six Million Swindle""

1. Emigration was the Jewish solution by the Nazis.
2. No Jews were gassed.
3. The unaccounted for Jews, presumably all six million, disappeared in Soviet Russian territory, not German.
4. The Jews that the Nazis killed were executed as spies, criminals, and subversives.
5. To claim the truth, Israel should have opened is archives.
6. All of the evidence shown to support the death of six million Jews is based on misquoted Nazis and Nazi documents
7. The accusers must prove the six million dead Jews.
8. Historians and scholars vary greatly as to the actual number of victims. [14]

Mr. Austin App joined efforts to revitalize denial of the Holocaust's occurrence in the 1980s and 1990s and mainstream its tenets. He joined such deniers as Arthur Butz, Bradley Smith, and Robert Faurisson, together with the Institute for Historical Review, attempting to give credibility to Holocaust denial.

The Institute for Historical Review (IHR) was founded by Willis Carto in 1978 is Costa Mesa, California. As Holocaust denial has become a propaganda cornerstone of organized racism, it is promoted by racist groups and organizations such as IHR. IHR attempts to re-write the history of World War II in favor of Germany and its allies and present 30s and 40s Nazism in a favorable light. IHR is inherently Anti-Semitic as the Liberty Lobby is quasi Neo-Nazi. The Liberty Lobby is now defunct having gone bankrupt in the early 2000s.

Willis A. Carto

Carto was the founder of the Anti-Semitic organization known as Liberty Lobby which went bankrupt in 2001. On the outside the group advertised itself as a political advocacy organization dedicated to advancing policies in line with the U.S. Constitution and the principles of Conservatism. What it really was embraced virulent Anti-Semitic views which kept alive organized Anti-Semitism as a

INTRODUCTION

political movement from the 50s through the 70s. He has stated: "Hitler's defeat was the defeat of Europe and America." In its newspaper, "The Spotlight," advertisements were printed for openly Neo-Nazi groups and their books. Carto still runs the Barnes Review founded in 1994. The publication "The Spotlight" is now defunct, but Carto and others are involved with a newspaper called "The American Free Press."

Willis Allison Carto is very connected to the radical, Anti-Semitic forces and is considered the most influential professional Anti-Semite in America. He shuns attention by the media and don't expect to view him in any interviews. He has been involved with many Anti-Semitic propaganda publications. Two of them, "American Mercury" and "Washington Observer Newsletter" are now defunct. During the 60s Carto produced racist, Nazi-tinged articles in the now also defunct "Western Destiny," and Noontide Press currently publishing anti-Jewish, pro-Nazi books.

A book published by Noontide, Parker Yockey's "Imperium" shaped Carto's Anti-Semitic, pro-Nazi mindset. The book was dedicated to Adolph Hitler and its 35-page introduction was written by Carto himself. Yockey's book glorifies Hitler who was admired by him and gives a re-statement of Nazi doctrine. Yockey denounced "The Church-

State-Nation-People-Race of the Jews" as "distorters of culture" [15]

The ideology of Yockey permeated the anti-Jewish propaganda of the Liberty Lobby and was the driving force behind the Institute for Historical Review (IHR) and the Populist Party. Even under oath at lawsuit proceedings in 1979, Carto testified of his continuing allegiance to Yockey's Neo-Nazi philosophy.

Carto's Anti-Semitism can be shown in his many quotes, such as:

> "If Satan himself, with all of his superhuman genius and diabolical ingenuity at his command, had tried to create a permanent disintegration and force for the destruction of the nations, he could have done no better than to invent the Jews."

Liberty Lobby published its newspaper, "The Spotlight" weekly had articles suggesting that Auschwitz victims were cremated to control typhoid, that the "gas changers" were actually life-saving delousing showers, that the "Diary of Anne Frank" was a hoax, and that Jews created the six million number to convince the United Nations to support the creation of Israel.

In August of 1994 it was announced in the "Spotlight" that a new publication was being

INTRODUCTION

launched by Liberty Lobby. This was called "The Barnes Review" and would be devoted to historical revisionism, or just plain Denialism. "The Barnes Review" is named after the 20th Century revisionist historian Harry Elmer Barnes.

Harry Elmer Barnes

Harry E. Barnes taught history at Columbia University from 1918-1929. Barnes believed that even if all the charges and atrocities against the Nazis were true, the allies and their behavior were not any better.

Often a moral equivalency is made by deniers that the suffering of ethnic Germans expelled from the Sudetenland, located in Czechoslovakia was equal to or worse than the Nazi extermination of European Jews. This is a theme repeated over and over by Barnes, as if it would make it true. In "Revisionism: A key to Peace," written in 1966 he said:

> "Even if one were to accept the most extreme and exaggerated indictment of Hitler and the National Socialists for their activities after 1939 made by anybody fit to remain outside a mental hospital, it is most alarmingly easy to demonstrate that the atrocities of the allies in the same period were more numerous as to victims and were carried out for the most part of methods more brutal and painful than that alleged extermination in gas ovens."

Barnes called the total blaming of Nazi Germany for its crimes as a historical "blackout." How dare the world blame Germany and defame its national character and conduct. He continued to cover up for Nazi Germany by trying to point out that atrocities committed by the allies were more brutal and numerous than the most extreme allegations made against the Germans.

Barnes, in 1964 wrote "Zionist Fraud" published in the Anti-Semitic "The American Mercury" in which he stated:

> "The courageous author (Rassinier) lays the chief blame for misrepresentation on those whom we must call the swindlers of the crematoria, the Israeli politicians who derive billions of marks from non-existent, mythical, and imaginary cadavers, whose numbers have been reckoned in an unusually distorted and dishonest manner."

Barnes went so far as to claim that Germany was the victim of aggression in 1914 and again in 1939. He thought that the Holocaust was just more propaganda to justify a war against Germany. He kept repeating that the world makes two false claims about World War II; that Germany started the war and that the Nazis executed the Holocaust.

Barnes says that historical "blackout" presents a one-sided view that only Nazis did

INTRODUCTION

dark, horrible things during World War II and contributes to an adolescent naivety by Americans to Germany's wartime crimes. Who knows, that may have been true if Britain and the United States had not participated in the war and exposed all the German crimes. That leads to the accusation by Barnes that "court historians" covered up all allied atrocities and war crimes never to see the light of day. He then moved on to assert that there were no Nazi death camps and that all the evidence showing gas chambers was all somehow manufactured to keep the public from becoming bored.

Barnes wrote:

> "What is deemed important today is not whether Hitler started war in 1939, or whether Roosevelt was responsible for Pearl Harbor, but the number of prisoners were allegedly done to death in the concentration camps operated in Germany during the war. These camps were first presented as those in Germany, such as Dachau, Belsen, Buchenwald, Sachsenhausen, and Dora, but it was demonstrated that there had been no systematic extermination in those camps. Attention was then moved on to Auschwitz, Treblinka, Belzec, Chelmno, Jonowska, Tarnow, Ravensbruck, Mauthausen, Breznia, and Birkenau, which did not exhaust the list that appears to have been extended as needed. [16]

In 1962, German historian Martin Brozat wrote to clarify the confusion over the differences between concentration camps and death camps. Concentration camps were places where inmates were mistreated and over-worked but were not subject to annihilation. Death camps were specifically built to exterminate their inmates. Dachau, a German concentration camp, did not have a functioning gas chamber until one was built there shortly before the end of the war and was never used. There were many concentration camps inside Germany but all of the German death camps were located in Nazi occupied Poland. The confusion in peoples' minds between the two types of camps, and about Dachau Camp was aiding early Holocaust deniers like Paul Rassinier, David Hoggan, and Barnes. It was Elmer Barnes who made a big deal that Dachau had no functioning gas chamber. In the same way, Barnes denied that the Einsatzgruppen murdered millions of Jews in the Soviet Union, and instead argued that the Einsatzgruppen were 'battling guerilla warfare behind the lines." [17]

Barnes went on to show how the Weimar Republic fought against the guilt imposed on Germany for starting World War I, with the German Government of Konrad Adenauer which accepted responsibility for starting

INTRODUCTION

World War II. Accepting German responsibility for the Holocaust set off Barnes to accusations opposing the Truth. Barnes became very vehement in his opposition of succeeding German governments, "groveling" and being "subservient" to the Jews. He also thought it was false for Jews to point out that they have been victims of Anti-Semitism for centuries. He also thought that to hold and express this view of the Jews was to be unjustly labeled as being Anti-Semitic. He believes that the "smotherout" is totally unjust. That is the view that the annihilation of the Jews overwhelms anything else that could be considered atrocities by the other side other than the Nazis.

Deborah Lipstadt in her book "Denying the Holocaust" names Barnes as the main link between the early revisionists, (re-evaluating German responsibility for World War I) and the modern Holocaust deniers. He always argued that the Holocaust never happened or was completely exaggerated by allied propaganda and Jewish politics. He was at first accepted by 1920s German government for his views excusing Germany from the guilt of starting World War I. But Barnes did not go along with West German Post-War Holocaust responsibility and has allied himself ever since with the Anti-Semite deniers. He has only added onto the resurging assault on truth and memory of such a black mark on mankind from the 20th Century. Having gained hearings in respectable areas these denial activities, though irrational, seek to gain a firm footing.

Before leaving the Holocaust denial part of Anti-Semitism, one other aspect of it should be mentioned, that of Islamic Negationism.

Islamic Negationism

Negationism is the denial of known historical facts. There may not be an officially stated policy of Muslim denial of the Holocaust, but they surely have unstated ones that are used to advantage. None of them will deny the Holocaust denial movement; that is, no public statements as such are forthcoming form Islam governments or terror outlets. If anything, the feeling is that the topic itself should not be allowed to make any forward progress as they attempt themselves to annihilate the Jews in their own fashion.

The Islamists just hate Jews, this is the reason, the whole foundation for their own existence. It is their religious duty from birth to hate the Jews.

But the Arabs at large in the world have followed in their support of negationism. In 1976 the Saudi representative at the United

INTRODUCTION

Nations made a speech in which he denied that he Holocaust had actually taken place.[18]

A young Iraqi spy wrote in his memoirs that he learned all about the "Jewish Conspiracy" and about Hitler's Third Reich, but nothing at all about the Holocaust.[19]

Muslims have some respect for Fascism and Mussolini. Muslims served the Fascist Ustashi's in Croatia and murdered Jews there. The Tartars, Kalmuks, Balkars, Chechens, and Ingoosh, all Muslim nations within the Soviet Union fought alongside the Nazis. The Muslims re-stated in post-war writings Nazi propaganda against the Jews. The Muslims just hate Jews wherever they find them.

In 1989 Ausaf Saied Vasfi, published out of Pakistan, an article feeding the hatred by Muslims of the Jews, stating two sources from which Zionism spring: The Talmud and the Protocols of the Elders. The Talmud is the chief Jewish scripture and directly orients the Jewish religion, Judaism. They seek a pluralistic interpretation of the texts, and accept them all including the literal. The difference today is that with the Talmud, Judaism seeks to transcend its exclusionist origins. Their interpretation puts the emphasis on intellectual investigation which they feel makes the Jewish community such a cradle of powerful minds. [20]

For this they are the target of hatred of the Arabs.

The Protocols of the Elders, as propaganda feeding the theory of the Jewish conspiracy will be covered upcoming. Suffice it to say that the theory feeds absurd notions such as the Kemalist revolution in Turkey was planned and carried out by international Jewry, and that the Bolshevik Revolution in Russia was also engineered by the Jews.

Hezbollah and Hamas, two Iranian backed terrorist groups, were to attend the negationist conference in Sweden until the Swedish government put a halt to the meeting. Saudi Arabia is the chief negationist supporter for activity in the West. Iranian embassies have been distributing negationist and anti-Jewish publications. Most, if not all, Arab nations sponsor negationist initiatives, but it is just intrinsically a part of Islam as a religion to be Anti-Semitic so as to carry out the dictates of their founder Mohammed. He targeted Jews from the beginning for rejecting Islam and for a sin worse than any: The Jews had deleted all references to Mohammed from their Scriptures.

Shylock

Another deeply ingrained menace that is still with us today portrays the stereotypical pattern of Anti-Semitism that can express

INTRODUCTION

itself at any time and in any place. It is especially present among the elite of the world. A stereotype is defined as something conforming to a fixed or general pattern. It is a standardized mental picture that is held in common by members of a group and that represents an oversimplified opinion, affective attitude, or uncritical judgment. (Webster)

Not many qualify as an oversimplified opinionated representative of any group as well as Vice-President Joe Biden who said: "People would come to him and talk about what was happening to them in terms of foreclosures, in terms of bad loans that were being, - I mean, these shylocks who took advantage of these women and men while overseas." [21]

This is another example of Biden's reverse euphemisms that are entering the vocabulary and becoming known as "Bidenisms". These are usually very offensive or stupid remarks made that need to be excused and forgotten. The Lord said, "...for out of the abundance of the heart the mouth speaketh." (Matthew 12:34). Christians know to be more aware of the words that come out of the mouth for the Lord told us that our words will judge us. Some, or most, that are in the public eye and ear haven't learned that lesson. One can surely tell what is in the heart of Joe Biden, especially if one has followed closely his sayings," Bidenisms", for the last few decades. It is too bad that these sayings are not more widely covered in our pusillanimous media today. Instead the costine press seeks only to cozen the people about the character of such a curmudgeon.

It was William Shakespeare who universalized the Jewish villain's character in the play "The Merchant of Venice." It was Shylock, a Jew, who was portrayed as the ruthless loan shark remembered for his demand of a "pound of flesh" from the merchant Antonio if he did not repay a loan. Shylock represents a medieval stereotype of Jews and is etched into the world's psyche as an offensive characterization to be hated and scorned to this day. [22] To refer to such a cant which slanders the whole race of Jews shows a callous degree of sophistry that is acceptable as truth today.

The point is that by loosely throwing around such offensively provocative terms, it shows once again how Anti-Semitic and stereotypical the whole human race can become. This is just another hurdle that the Jews must be forced to overcome. By using the term Shylock as a synonym for loan shark it stigmatizes and identifies Jews in opprobrious appellations not deserving.

INTRODUCTION

English society in Elizabethan times has been described as Anti-Semitic. [23]

It happened that in the twelfth century, England, Germany, and France were developing a Judeophobia that was considerably violent with accusations that Jews were involved in ritual murder, profanation of the host, and the poisoning of wells. It would not be hard to state that as a result of these types of prejudices, Jews found it difficult to fit in with society. These attitudes formed some of the foundations of Anti-Semitism in the 20th Century.

English Jews had been evicted in 1290 and not permitted to return until the time of Cromwell. On the Elizabethan stage Jews were hideously portrayed with having hooked noses and bright red wigs and depicted as rapacious usurers. Usury is the lending of money for interest usually at exorbitant rates. Shylock has come to mean to lend money at an exorbitant rate, as a usurer, thus usurers are Jews. Jews, or Shylocks, were usually depicted as evil, deceptive, and greedy.

Jews in the 1600s in Venice faced the death penalty if they did not wear red hats in public for easy identification. Jews were forced to live in ghettos and had to pay their guards for their protection. "The Merchant of

Venice" is seen by some to be the illustration of Anti-Semitic prejudice of that day.

There is no mistaking, the character Shylock has come from the pen to extract feelings of greed, avarice, and even sympathy from the world. No matter how he is viewed, the overall portraying of the Jew in the world has suffered. It has led to inhumane and insensitive treatment of an entire people to the intent of complete annihilation in the minds of the evil. Shakespeare illuminates the cry of the Jewish people at the world's mercy:

> Hath not a Jew eyes? Hath not a Jew hands,
>
> organs, dimensions, senses, affections, passions;
>
> fed with the same food, hurt with the same weapons,
>
> subject to the same diseases,
>
> heal'd by the same means,
>
> warm'd and cool'd by the same winter and
>
> summer
>
> as a Christian is? If you prick us, do we not
>
> bleed?
>
> If you tickle us, do we not laugh? If you poison
>
> us,

INTRODUCTION

> do we not die? And if you wrong us, shall we not
>
> revenge?
>
> If we are like you in the rest, we will resemble
>
> you in that.
>
> If a Jew wrong a Christian, what is his humility?
>
> Revenge. If a Christian wrong a Jew, what
>
> should his
>
> Sufferance be by a Christian example? Why,
>
> revenge.
>
> The villainy you teach me, I will execute,
>
> and it shall go hard but I will better the
>
> Instruction.
>
> Act III, Scene I, The Merchant of Venice.

Shakespeare's play has either intentional or unintentional Anti-Semitic overtones but has been made use of by Anti-Semites since it was first performed. The prevailing view in England at the time was of Shylock being an incredibly cruel Jew. This permeated English society and has repercussions up to this present day. The effect has spread throughout the world and has caused immeasurable trouble for the Jews. The play, and thus the depiction of the cruel Jew, was used for propaganda purposes throughout Nazi Germany and Nazi-occupied territory.

Throughout English literature and into the literature of other English-speaking countries, the representation of Jews bears the strong mark of "The Merchant of Venice," and Shylock. The Jew is shown as being cruel, covetous, deviant, deceptive, and greedy. To use the term "Shylock" to describe an action is at best unfortunate and serves only as a perpetuation of a cruel myth.

Consequences

There are severe consequences for targeting a whole race of people, such as the Jews. An example of today's persecution of God's people by a Satanic organization is a video circulated by the terrorist group Al-Qaeda. They are represented by a group of "resisters of occupation in the occupied West Bank and Jerusalem." It shows to Palestinians how to stab a Jewish person in a way that ensures their speedy death. The men in the video are dressed in the Keffiyeh headscarf which was made popular by the late terrorist, Yasser Arafat. The teaching demonstrates walking up to an Israeli citizen, stabbing them and using a twisting action in order to inflict maximum damage.

INTRODUCTION

There has been a rampant rise in such attacks of Arabs against Israeli Jews. In November 2014 two Palestinian terrorists stabbed to death four Rabbis in a Jerusalem Synagogue. The Religion of Peace Jihadis left 8 wounded in the attack. Hamas supported the actions and threatened, "There will be more revolution in Jerusalem, and more uprising." Using stereotypes and through inaction these horrific events are here to stay.

Support for Israel

Christian support for Israel must not wane, but remain strong in the face of such threatening danger. There was an article posted online that listed 10 ways to support Israel:

Be active online. Speak up!

Buy Israeli products

Join a pro-Israeli organization

Teach your friends and family about Israel

Pray...

Attend a pro-Israel Rally

Visit Israel

Protest bias in the media

Education yourself so you can educate other

Fly the Israeli flag

These are just a few of the things Christians need to do to inform themselves and others. This paper is intended to teach and be a learning experience also. Other things would be to read the Bible, read other books by Jewish authors, as well as Christian authors. Two such books that are recommended would be, "Standing with Israel" by David Brog, and "In Defense of Israel" by John Hagee. Brog is a Jew and believes that we are witnessing today a Christian/Jewish reconciliation that has taken over two thousand years to emerge. He attempts to correct Jewish perceptions that they have harbored for a long period of time in regards to Christians. He approaches the subject as a staunch believer in Judaism and deeply believes that evangelical Christians who support Israel are the theological heirs of the righteous Gentiles who tried desperately to save Jews from the horrors of the Holocaust.

John Hagee exposes some of the common myths about the Jews and Israel in his book, "In Defense of Israel." Rev. Hagee has been publicly supporting Israel ever since organizing the Night to Honor Israel in September of 1981. In 2006 he formed Christians United for Israel (CUFI), a national organization standing in support of Israel and the Jewish people. The goals are worthy;

INTRODUCTION

having evangelicals become more aware of the Anti-Semitism being taught everywhere, developing a deep love toward Jewish people, standing together and influencing Washington on the supporting of Israel issue, and countering the threat of radical Islam to Judeo-Christian civilization.

Hagee has been to Jerusalem, to the Kotel or the Western Wall, the ancient retaining wall that dates from 516 B.C. This wall is what remains from the second Temple, which was totally destroyed by the Roman, Titus, in the attack and rampaging of the City of Jerusalem in 70 A.D. There are blue plastic chairs there for worshipers to sit in. He prayed amongst orthodox Jews who dress in a white shirt and long black coat over black trousers. They sport a full beard, wear a bead-trimmed yarmulke, or skullcap pinned to the top of their head. They use white and blue shawls across their shoulders, and rock back and forth when addressing almighty God. As a result of his visiting the Western Wall, Hagee was inspired to do everything in his power to bring Christians and Jews together. It is true that Christians from birth through seminary have never learned the whole truth about what the Jewish people have undergone through History. Most people have never been taught the truth about the Crusades, the Spanish Inquisition, or the Holocaust.

A Warning

Today there is a rising millennial generation of Christians, in their 20s and 30s that are abandoning traditional support for Israel. Anti-Israeli Palestinian "Christians," together with other American sympathizers, are trying to reach these millennials with a propaganda laden narrative seeking to weaken support for Israel. Although it is the position of this author to support Rev. Hagee in attempting to keep a high level of support of Israel at every age, there needs to be an understanding of who John Hagee is and what his charismatic stances are. This is not a reflection upon the work Hagee is doing to support Israel and should not be taken as any sort of personal attack. It is from the understanding that Rev. Hagee is no Fundamentalist and, therefore, some separation due to doctrinal differences must be cited. Also, it must be noted that some of his writing in his book, "In Defense of Israel" is being used in this book and must be considered separate from the man.

In 1994, while Hagee was serving in the pulpit at the Charismatic Trinity Church in San Antonio, Texas, he divorced his wife, resigned the pulpit and married a young woman in the congregation, Diana Castro. Custody for his two children was awarded to his ex-wife, Martha.

INTRODUCTION

NOTE: Most of this information on John Hagee culled from Plains Baptist Challenger, May 2006.

Depending on one's belief according to the qualifications to be in the pulpit, would be the interpretation of Paul in 1 Timothy 3:2 and Titus 1:6. Paul lists "husband of one wife" as the second qualification of being a pastor and being in the pulpit. The interpretation of "one wife at a time" is a foolhardy and iconoclastic misinterpretation of Holy Scripture. In conclusion, John Hagee is disqualified to be in the pulpit on the basis of his divorce and remarriage. Does he appear to take God at His word? Just turn on the television for the answer.

There are many things about the charismatic John Hagee that should trouble Fundamentalists. The whole charismatic movement is about tearing down walls and building bridges between the various religious groups, and John Hagee is no exception. In the year 2000 Hagee worked together with Jack Van Impe on the movie, Revelation. In 2002, Hagee endorsed Bill Bright's Global Pastors Network.

John Hagee believes in a Prosperity Gospel. In 1993 he appeared on the Praise-A-Thon on the Trinity Broadcast Network. He said on it, "poverty is caused by sin and disobeying the word of God." On another show he said, "Your income is controlled by your giving." Jesus told us that the poor would always be with us and taught heavenly rewards, not earthly prosperity.

> "Charge them that are rich in this world, that they be not high-minded, nor trust in uncertain riches, but in the living God, who giveth us richly all things to enjoy;" (1 Timothy 6:17).

In 2 Corinthians 8:2, Paul tells of the deep poverty of those in that church in Macedonia. Even in their deep poverty they gave liberally, and were still in their deep poverty after giving sacrificially. God gave them grace to give in sacrifice, rather than be rewarded financially.

A doctrine of the flesh rather than being Biblical, is the Positive Confession or name it and claim it doctrine. This states that any believer in Christ can bring anything into existence if enough faith is exercised along with verbal expression of confession. He goes along with the faith teachers by professing prosperity after speaking and acting on the Word of God. A Christian must remember to bring requests before the throne of God by faith, but it is the will of God which determines if the request will be granted and not our will.

One remarkable stance of John Hagee, in light of his work for Israel and the Jews is his believing in the Dual Covenant or Two

INTRODUCTION

Covenant doctrine. He denies this, but his words convict him on it. The Dual Covenant states that the Jews, in whole or in part, are saved not by the finished work of Jesus Christ, but by the fact that they are Jews.

> "Everyone else, whether Buddhist or Baha'i, needs to believe in Jesus...but not the Jews." John Hagee in an interview with the Houston Chronicle.

Wikipedia states:

> "Dual-Covenant theology is a liberal Christian view that holds that Jews may simply keep the Law of Moses because of the "everlasting covenant" (Genesis 17:13) between Abraham and God expressed in the Hebrew Bible, whereas Gentiles (those not Jews or Jewish proselytes) must convert to Christianity..."

It seems as if Rev. Hagee's staunch zealousness for the Jewish people and their cause has led him to err about salvation for Jews without the blood of Christ. Hagee further states that,

> "Jews already have a covenant with God that has never been replaced with Christianity."

There cannot be two separate methods of salvation instituted and provided by God.

Hagee comments further, from the April 30, 1988 Houston Chronicle he said:

> "I believe that every Gentile person can only come to God through the Cross of Christ. I believe that every Jewish person who lives in the light of the Torah, which is the Word of God, has a relationship with God and will come to redemption."

It is impossible to reject the Messiah, who is the Lord Jesus Christ, and still have a relationship with God through the Torah. When we look at the New Testament, with John the Baptist, the Apostles, the New Testament writers all being Jews, we need to question Hagee's soundness on this doctrine. Paul, as we shall see, had deep concern for the nation Israel being in a lost state. Roman's 10: 1-4 bears out the fact that the Jews' zeal for God is not faith and that they had not submitted to the righteousness of God. Jesus said that no man can come to the Father in salvation except by Jesus Christ (John 14:6). Jesus is saying that Jew and Gentile alike must be saved and come to God through him.

Conversion of Jews

Efforts to convert Jews to Christ and have them under the blood of Christ, is biblical. To give up on witnessing Christ to the Jews is a violation of the Great Commission given to the Church by Christ.

> *"Go ye therefore, and teach all nations..."* (Matthew 28:19); *"Go ye into all the world, and preach the gospel to every*

INTRODUCTION

creature." (Mark 16:15) *"and that repentance and remission of sins should be preached in his name among all nations, beginning at Jerusalem."* (Luke 24:47); *"...and ye shall be witnesses unto me both in Jerusalem, and in all Judea, and in Samaria, and unto the uttermost part of the earth."* (Acts 1:8). *Jesus said go unto the Jew and Gentile to every part of the Earth to preach the Gospel to all and that all would come to repentance and be baptized for the remission of sins. However, some have not received the Commission.*

NOTE: These examples are taken from O! Timothy Magazine by David Cloud, Vol. 20, Issue 8, 2003. Pp 17, 18.

In September 1988, Rabbi Andrew Baker said "Christian efforts to convert Jews have been abandoned by nearly all Catholic and mainstream Protestant denominations."

In June 1988, the Presbyterian Church USA approved a report stating that the Jews worship the same God as Christians and that they have an abiding covenant with that God.

In June of 1988 the United Church of Christ stated that Jews have an abiding covenant with God and that they do not have to believe the Gospel of Jesus Christ.

Also in June 1988, Pat Robertson, radical charismatic said that Jews go to heaven in relation to their own religion.

It was in April of 1987 Episcopal Bishop John Walker of Washington, D.C. said

> "If we truly believe that the Jews are the people of God, we should not lend support to groups that seek to convert Jews to Christianity."

The Augsburg (American Lutheran Church) Publishing House in a book claimed that the Jews are accepted by God without Jesus Christ.

Billy Graham is most likely the most popular evangelist in the last 100 years and is known in the past for his crusades. Before the 1987 crusade in Denver, Colorado, he made it clear to religious leaders there that,

> "to allay any fears that he would target Jews for conversion."

He also added,

> "It is my conviction that Christ is the way to God's forgiving love, but it ill behooves me to judge Jews as people lost to salvation."

In April 1958, Reinhold Niebuhr, a United Church of Christ professor at Apostate Union Theological Seminary, said that work to convert Jews is both "futile and wrong."

INTRODUCTION

Paul wrote in Romans 1:16:

> *"For I am not ashamed of the gospel of Christ: for it is the power of God unto salvation to everyone that believeth; To the Jew first, and also the Greek.,"*

Romans 3:19-24 tells us that the Mosaic covenant does not save anybody. No wonder John Hagee feels the way he does about the Jew and salvation. He follows a long list of those who believe that Jews are saved because they are Jews and Gentiles are saved because of the blood of Christ. It is true that Mr. Hagee's Christians' Unified for Israel, according to Mr. Morganstern, official spokesman for CUFI in Israel, has nothing to do with the Bible, and does not discuss Biblical things ever. CUFI is then to be regarded as a humanitarian organization, like United Way, and not as a group proclaiming Jesus or salvation to a lost country or world. It is little wonder that John Hagee is so popular in the country of Israel.

Be A Witness to the Jews

Paul wished for his Jewish compatriots to be saved. We will see that later. Jew and non-Jew must come to God by faith in Jesus Christ. God is no respector of persons.

> *"What then? Are we better than they? No, in no wise: for we have proved both*

> *Jews and Gentiles, that they are all under sin:"* (Romans 3:9)

There is only one way of salvation for the Jew or the Gentile. That is through the finished work of the Lord Jesus Christ on the Cross. By faith in Christ, this is the single plan of salvation for everyone.

You must realize that you are a sinner and that you need a Saviour. You cannot go to Heaven if you die in your sins.

> *"For all have sinned, and come short of the glory of God." (Romans 3:23)*

> *"The wicked shall be turned into hell, ..."* (Psalm 9:17a)

Agree with God that you are a sinner and change your mind about sin.

> *"And the times of this ignorance God winked at; but now commandeth all men everywhere to repent:"* (Acts 17:30)

Believe that the Lord Jesus Christ died for your sins so that you could be made free.

> *"For I delivered unto you first of all that which I also received, how that Christ died for our sins according to the scriptures; and that he was buried, and that he rose again the third day according to the scriptures:"* (1 Corinthians 15: 3.4).

Genuinely believe in and receive the Lord Jesus Christ as your Lord and Saviour.

INTRODUCTION

> *"For God so loved the World, that he gave his only begotten Son, that whosoever believeth in him should not perish, but have everlasting life."* (John 3:16)
>
> *"For with the heart man believeth unto righteousness; and with the mouth confession is made unto salvation."* (Romans 10:10).

Now the Gospel must be preached to every Jew in the world that Jesus Christ is Lord and Saviour. Along with Gentiles the message must be renewed with vigor to our Jewish friends.

The Purpose

The purpose of this volume then, is to encourage Christians and blinded Jews alike to educate, learn all about, support, pray for, and give respect to all Jews and the Nation of Israel in every way possible.

This is an immense subject and cannot be conceivably or thoroughly given justice here. The separate aspects of the history of Israel, its journey to the present day, its dispersion, the Anti-Semitic lies against it, supersessionism, will all be dealt with in relation to Israel's past, its present, and its future.

Let it be said that it is God that is still in control of events and is guiding Israel through its unbelief. It is Satan who is trying to destroy God's chosen earthly nation. The Bible tells us the sure outcome. The duty of Christians is to follow the commands of God in regards to Israel. Hopefully those will be clearer at the end of the journey. Do not allow Satan to deter God's desire to have Christians help in the spiritual needs of the Jews. Many Jews have found Jesus and are very glad that God has lifted that veil from their hearts and cause the scales to fall from their eyes.

We must not be quiet while Satan seeks to destroy Israel. The road is difficult for the Jew. It is illegal to witness to or hand out tracts to Jews in Jerusalem and throughout Israel. There are those that do no matter what, but they have to be careful. One can hand out tracts and witness in Turkey, but not Israel. It is not against the law in Turkey, but it could be dangerous. [24]

To the nations around us we must say, the Jews are God's people, so stand with them. To the Jew we say, Jesus is your Messiah, we serve Him. Come, serve Him with us. To this end this Tome is offered.

CHAPTER 1
A History of Ancient Israel

It should be viewed by the reader of the Bible that the fundamental material contained therein tells the history of the children and nation of Israel. This is no accident. Both the Old Testament and the New describe God's history with His people from covenant to Israel's future.

The first inklings of Israel begin in the Pentateuch which is succeeded by the accounts of Israel's history from the book of Joshua through the book of Esther. The historical books are Joshua, Judges, Ruth, I and II Samuel, I and II Kings, and I and II Chronicles, Ezra, Nehemiah, and Esther. These are the books from which we mainly derive our ancient history of Israel.

Thomas Jefferson said about the Bible, "I have always said, and always will say, that the studious perusal of the Sacred Volume will make better citizens, better husbands, and better fathers." What better advice do we have as we observe radical children burning and looting, killing their own babies, and divorcing for any reason.

Daniel Webster said,

> "I have read it (the Bible) through many times. I now make a practice of going through it once a year. It is the book of all others for lawyers as well as divines. I pity the man who cannot find in it a rich supply of thought and rules for conduct."

The Bible was written by about forty different writers, authored by God, and given over a time period of approximately fifteen hundred years.

To Make a Nation

> "For whatsoever things were written aforetime were written for our learning," (Romans 15:4)

What we have written in the Old Testament in our King James Bible, God gave us as examples for our learning all the principles, commandments, and warnings. God's giving of the history of Israel ranges throughout the Bible, consisting in its past thru the future. Israel's beginning up to its present starts with the Patriarchs; Abraham, Isaac, Jacob, and Joseph.

The book of Genesis is the beginning of beginnings. The first eleven chapters contain God's creation, Adam and Eve, the fall of man, the Flood, and the Tower of Babel with the dividing of peoples. Sin is mentioned for the first time as well as the Sabbath, marriage, family, murder, sacrifice, race, languages, redemption, and cities. The first eleven chapters span some two thousand years. From Genesis 12 to Genesis 50 cover about three hundred and fifty years. This is where the start of the history of Israel shall begin, with Abraham, Isaac, Jacob, and Joseph.

God's Call To Abraham

> *"Now the Lord had said unto Abram, get thee out of thy country, and from thy kindred, and from thy father's house, unto a land that I will shew thee:"* (Genesis 12:1)
>
> Now Abram was Abraham's name until God said *"thy name shall be Abraham; for a father of many nations have I made thee."* (Genesis 17:5).

Terah was Abraham's father. He took Abraham, Lot, and Sarai (Sarah) from the city of Ur of the Chaldees to Haran in Canaan.

Abram, or Abraham is the first great patriarch or father of Israel. A patriarch is one of the three great progenitors of Israel, namely, Abraham, Isaac, and Jacob. Joseph will also be considered, for he is important in the Godly formation of the nation of Israel.

The Abrahamic Covenant

God calls Abraham to make to him a threefold promise that will form and give the foundation to the nation of Israel forever. God said unto Abraham, get thee, "unto a land that

I will shew thee." (Genesis 12:1) That is the first part of God's promise. The next part of the promise is that God through Abraham will make a great nation which is to be Israel.

God is then going to make Abraham a blessing, through whom all others will be blessed.

> "And I will make of thee a great nation, and I will bless thee, and make thy name great; and thou shalt be a blessing." (Genesis 12:2)

Abraham, and Israel, yet to be formed, will be a great nation. Abraham will be considered by all to be the father of Israel, great, and blessed and guided by God.

> "And I will bless them that bless thee, and curse him that curseth thee: and in thee shall all families of the earth be blessed." (Genesis 12:3)

Those that know and are of Abraham are blessed. Throughout the history of the earth the blessing and curse will go. Those countries that are established and bless Israel will be blessed by God and flourish and grow. But those who curse Israel and beat her down will be cursed and die. Many nations have come and are no more as a result of this promise by God. God blessed Abraham all through his life and the ones who blessed him were also blessed. God will make good on the first part of His promise, as He will place Israel

CHAPTER 1: A HISTORY OF ISRAEL

permanently and forever after he deals with the Gentiles during the Tribulation. God gave Israel over 300,000 square miles of land which they will occupy during the Millennium. It will not be granted by the United Nations, where they are now, but God will give it to them on His timetable.

God promised Abraham, his name meaning "father of many," a son to be born from Sarah to be a great nation of people. It was a mark of remarkable faith on the part of Abraham since he and Sarah both were old at that time. Abraham, Sarah, and Lot departed Horan and came to Canaan. As a result of a famine Abraham and Sarah passed into Egypt. They returned to Canaan where Abraham and Lot chose where they would settle. It was Lot's misfortune to choose to live in Sodom, where the, "men of Sodom were wicked and sinners before the Lord exceedingly." (Genesis 13:13).

Again the Lord promised to give to Abraham and his descendants all the land which he could see and to multiply his seed, "as the dust of the earth:" (Genesis 13:16a). Abraham was called the Hebrew, for he was the first Hebrew.

> *"And there came one that had escaped, and told Abram the Hebrew;"* (Genesis 14:13a)

Israel will be restored in her land, promised by God, at the return of the Lord Jesus Christ as King under the Davidic Covenant.

> "And David my servant shall be kind over then;...and they shall swell in the land, ...even they, and their children, and their children's children forever, and my servant David shall be their prince forever." (Ezekiel 37: 24a, 25)

> "And God said, Sarah thy wife shall bear thee a son indeed; and thou shalt call his name Isaac: and I will establish my covenant with him for an everlasting covenant, and with his seed after him." (Genesis 17:19)

The Covenant that God gave to Abraham in Genesis 12:1-3, was confirmed to him in Genesis 13:14-17; again in Genesis 15:5-7; and also in Genesis 17:2-8.

The Abrahamic Covenant consists of seven parts. The first is, "I will make of thee a great nation." In the natural, "as the dust of the earth." (Genesis 13:16). In the spiritual way; "Look now toward heaven...so shall thy seed be." (Genesis 15:5). "Know ye therefore that they which are of faith, the same are the children of Abraham." (Galatians 3:7). The covenant is also fulfilled through the children of Ismael, the child of the flesh; "and as for Ismael, I have heard thee: Behold, I have blessed him, and will make him fruitful, and

CHAPTER 1: A HISTORY OF ISRAEL

will multiply him exceedingly;" (Genesis 17:20).

The next part "I will bless thee" was fulfilled in two ways: temporally and spiritually. Temporally, "and the LORD hath blessed my master greatly; and he has become great: and he hath given him flocks, and herds, and silver, and gold, and menservants, and maidservants, and camels, and asses," (Genesis 24:35). The spiritual blessing is given in Genesis 15:6, "and he believed the LORD; and he counted it to him for righteousness."

The third part of the covenant to Abraham simply states, "and make thy name great" which is great to Jews and Christians alike to this very day.

Number four, "and thou shalt be a blessing" is found fulfilled in Galatians 3:14, "that the blessing of Abraham might come on the Gentiles through Jesus Christ; that we might receive the promise of the Spirit through faith." The promise of blessing to Abraham is only made possible because Christ has redeemed us with His blood when he hung on the Cross of Calvary. We can receive the blessing of redemption by faith as Abraham did.

The fifth and sixth parts go hand in hand with each other. "I will bless them that bless thee, and curse him that curseth thee." We see the blessing of God that was on those individuals and nations that blessed Abraham and Israel. The country of England is one when that nation was a world empire based on belief in the King James Bible and the God behind it. That has faded now as England has turned its back on God. The same can be said for the United States which has been blessed with Godly freedom as it remained Israel's best friend. Sadly, we are in decline now as we have been turning our backs on God and Israel. Through this third dispersion of the Jews people and nations that have persecuted Jews and Israel have not fared very well as opposed to them that have protected Jews and Israel.

>"and the Lord thy God will put all these curses upon thine enemies, and on them that hate thee, which persecuted thee." (Deuteronomy 30:7)

>"Thine hand shall be lifted up upon thine adversaries, and all thine enemies shall be cut off." (Micah 5:9)

>"Then shall he answer them,... Inasmuch as ye did it not to one of the least of these, ye did it not to me. And these shall go away into everlasting punishment: but the righteous unto life eternal." (Matthew 25: 45, 46)

The final part of the covenant is, "In thee shall all families of the earth be blessed." This

CHAPTER 1: A HISTORY OF ISRAEL

is the promise fulfilled in Abraham's seed, the Lord Jesus Christ. "Jesus said unto them, verily, verily, I say unto you, before Abraham was, I am." (John 8:58) Jesus Christ is the seed of the woman, the promise of a Saviour in Genesis 3:15, "and I will put enmity between thee and the woman, and between thy seed and her seed; it shall bruise thy head, and thou shalt bruise his heel."

Abraham, the original Hebrew, is the great patriarch of Israel. He is the Christian's spiritual father.

> *"What shall we say then that Abraham our father, as pertaining to the flesh, hath found?"*
>
> *"Therefore it is of faith, that it might be by grace; to the end the promise might be sure to all the seed;...which is of the faith of Abraham; who is the father of us all."* (Romans 4:1, 16)

All this was done, and God chose Abraham to be the Hebrew royal line by which the Redeemer of the entire race would come.

ISAAC

> *"And I will bless her, and give thee a son also of her: Yea, I will bless her, and she shall be a mother of nations; kings of people shall be of her."* (Genesis 17:16)

Sarah, at her old age of ninety, will be a mother of nations. God already said to

Abraham,"...and thou shalt be a father of many nations." (Genesis 17:4b)

> *"For it is written, that Abraham had two sons, the one by a bondmaid, the other by a freewoman."* (Galatians 4:22)

As Sarah was exalted by God, Christian holy women are considered now as daughters of Sarah, "Even as Sarah obeyed Abraham, calling him Lord: whose daughters ye are" (1 Peter 3:6)

So the next in line of the Messiah would be from,

"Sarah thy wife shall bear thee a son indeed; and thou shalt call his name Isaac:" (Genesis 17:19).

Ismael had been born to Abraham but God said,

> *"My covenant will I establish with Isaac,"* (Genesis 17:21a).

This means that the spiritual things that God has intended, the birth of the Messiah and the salvation to both the Jews and the Gentiles would continue through Isaac.

The birth of Isaac was one of many that we can point to as being a foreshadowing of the birth of Christ. Sarah bore Abraham a son named Isaac, "at the set time of which God had spoken to him. (Genesis 21:2).

CHAPTER 1: A HISTORY OF ISRAEL

> *"But when the fullness of the time was come, God sent forth his Son, made of a woman, made under the law."* (Galatians 4:4)

Isaac was a son that God promised to Abraham. God promised a son to Israel to be the Messiah (Isaiah 7:14). Isaac was named by God to Abraham before he was born. (Genesis 17:19). The same was true of our Lord,

> *"And she shall bring forth a son, and thou shalt call his name Jesus: for he shall save his people from their sins."* (Matthew 1:21).

At a young age Isaac was the object of an act which looks forward to the sacrifice of Christ at Calvary. It happened to be Abraham's final testing of his faith and obedience to his loving God. In the sacrifice of Isaac there is the supernatural similarity to our Lord Jesus Christ. It was going to take a sacrifice to save sinners, and this is the illustration here. Isaac was not sacrificed in the real sense, but Abraham's obedience to fulfill God's will was a work of faith. Abraham exercised his faith he had in his heart. (Genesis 15:6).

God tells Abraham to take Isaac, his only son, to be offered. Jesus Christ is the only begotten Son of God. (John 1:14, 18; 3:16,18). *"And get thee into the Land of*

Moriah;" (Genesis 22:2). Isaac was to be offered upon one of the mountains there. This is supposed to mean all the mountains of Jerusalem, comprehending Mount Gihon or Calvary, the Mount of Sion and of Acra.[1]

This mountain ridge, which includes Mt. Moriah is thought to be the place where the temple was built later, and where Golgotha is, where our Lord Jesus Christ was crucified. This is the same general area where Abraham offered Isaac. Abraham accepted the fact that God wanted Isaac offered, but he also believed God would raise him back up from the dead.

> *"Accounting that God was able to raise him up, even from the dead;"* (Hebrews 11:19a)

Isaac was forty years old when his father, Abraham, took measures to find Isaac a wife. Abraham did not want any one of the daughters of the Canaanites to be a wife to his son. These of the Canaanites were devoted to slavery and under the curse, so for the heir of the promise of God's son to be joined to one under a curse would be inconsistent. Abraham's servant was to go to the land of Haran, to his kindred, for a wife and not return to Canaan where there abounded idolatry and paganism. Rebekah, a cousin of Isaac, became his wife.

CHAPTER 1: A HISTORY OF ISRAEL

"And Isaac brought her into his mother Sarah's tent, and took Rebekah, and she became his wife;" (Genesis 24: 67a)

When Rebekah sees Isaac afar off, and she sees him face to face, is a picture of us who have not seen the Lord, but we love Him. *"Therefore she took a veil, and covered herself."* (Genesis 24:65b). As the bride of Christ we have been covered by the righteousness of Christ who was delivered for our sins, raised for our justification so that we are covered in Christ's righteousness in order for us to be able to stand before God.

Isaac was 60 years old when Rebekah gave birth to Esau and Jacob. As it happened one day Esau came in weak from working in the field and exchanged his birthright for some pottage. There were some special rights to the birthright in those days. These would include: authority and superiority over the rest of the family; a double portion of the paternal inheritance; the peculiar benediction of the father; the priesthood before that of the family of Aaron.[2]

Jacob, having supplanted Esau of his rights of primo-geniture by his cunning and deception, gets his next chance to display his nature. Isaac, who was a successful farmer, (Genesis 6:12), was old and feeble and prepared for the blessing of his two sons. Savory meat was to be prepared by Esau for

Isaac and the reasons for that may include: eating together for the binding of the covenant or blessing that was to occur; that a certain rite would be necessary to convey the blessings; to invigorate or strengthen Isaac for the blessing to be administered.[3]

Jacob fooled Isaac by wearing skins of Esau and stole his blessing. It was the design of God that the elder should serve the younger but it was not to be brought about in his manner. But now Jacob had taken away Esau's birthright and blessing, and Esau wants to kill Jacob. Jacob flees to Padan-aram to hide out and stay with his uncle Laban. Along the way he "lighted upon a certain place," (Genesis 28:11) where God confirms to him the blessing of Abraham which Isaac had prayed.

> "And give thee the blessing of Abraham, to thee, and to thy seed with thee: that thou mayest inherit the land wherein thou art a stranger, which God gave to Abraham." (Genesis 28:4)

Jacob journeyed on to the country beyond the Euphrates, exactly where Isaac's wife Rebekah had come from. There he went to work for seven years for the hand of Rachel, who was very beautiful. At the end of seven years Laban made ready the marriage feast. However, Laban brought the oldest daughter Leah to Jacob, and in the morning discovery of

CHAPTER 1: A HISTORY OF ISRAEL

this was made known to the unsuspecting Jacob. He had been had by his uncle Laban since in their country,

> "It must be so done in our country, to give the younger before the first-born." (Genesis 29:26).

According to the Code of Gentoo Laws, Chap. XV., section 1, p204[4], this was the eastern Mesopotamian law.

So, Jacob must work another seven years to secure the hand of Rachel, whom he truly loved. He served Laban an additional seven years for a total of around twenty years. During this time Leah gives birth to Reuban, her firstborn son. She also gives birth to Simeon, Levi, and Judah who was the kingly line from which comes the Lord Jesus Christ according to the flesh. Reuban loses his firstborn portion because of sin, and Levi was the priestly line. Besides these four boys, Leah also gives birth to Issachar and Zebulun. Bilhah, Rachel's handmaid has Gad and Naphtali. Zilpah, Lelah's handmaid gives birth to Gad and Asher. Rachel's two sons are Joseph and Benjamin. These twelve sons will make up the twelve tribes of the nation Israel.

On the way back to his country and an encounter with his brother Esau, a change is happening inside of Jacob. He is afraid of what Esau may do to him and his family and cries:

> "I am not worthy of the least of all the mercies, and of all the truth," (Genesis 32:10a)

God answered him and assured Jacob,

> "I will surely do thee good,..." (Genesis 32:12a).

As soon as we start reaching out to God as he is showing us our pitiful state of sinfulness, he responds and moves toward us as sinners in need.

Jacob takes his wives, his maidservants, and eleven sons and sent them on to the meeting with Esau.

> "And Jacob was left alone; and there wrestled a man with him until the breaking of the day." (Genesis 32:24)

Jacob struggled with the man who was none other than the pre-incarnate Christ. He did not let him go and demanded a blessing. This is known as a Theophany, or Christophany, which is a visible manifestation of God in the person of the pre-incarnate Christ. The Jewish religion does not believe in the Trinity, so Theophanies in the Old Testament use other descriptions, such as "the angel of the Lord." (Genesis 16:7), or "a man" such as in this verse. (Genesis 32:24). Christ changed Jacob the usurper to Israel, a prince with a new nature and with power with God and man. Jacob, Israel will emerge from the

CHAPTER 1: A HISTORY OF ISRAEL

encounter with Christ as a man of faith up to his death. It is through the Lord Jesus Christ that we are changed from men and women of the flesh to ones of faith. We are victorious not by our fighting and struggling against the Lord, but by yielding to Him just as Jacob did. This is another example of things that happened to those in the Old Testament that are written as examples for our admonition (Nouthesia, instruction) (1 Corinthians 10:11).

The twelve, now still eleven, along with Jacob were nomadic shepherds with a range from near the plain of Esdraelon in the north-west and the borders of Syrian territory in the north-east down to the edge of the country included in the Egyptian Kingdom.[5]

Jacob's seventeen year old son, Joseph, was feeding the sheep and brought to his father an evil report about his brothers. Jacob played favorite son with Joseph, so all of this did not sit well with his older brothers. Add to that the coat which had sleeves in it which let him stand out among all the rest. On top of all this hatred is a dream Joseph has which he says that he will eventually rule over them all. A second dream gives them an image of a similar report as in Revelation 12:1 which represents the nation of Israel. This is the very beginning of the nation of Israel at its budding. They all understood the dream, no interpretation was needed, only a disbelief.

> *"And his brethren envied him; but his father observed the saying,"* (Genesis 37:11)

With Joseph there is no other prominent figure in Scripture who is a type of the Lord Jesus Christ in his person or experiences. A type as used in the Bible is a symbol, or an illustration or a picture. Joseph is a picture of the Lord Jesus Christ in at least six ways according to Dr. Vernon McGee:

1. Both Joseph and Christ born by special divine intervention of God. (Genesis 30.22; Luke 1:35)

2. Joseph loved by Jacob. Jesus Christ loved by the Father and his beloved Son.

3. Joseph was set apart by his sleeved coat. Jesus was separate from sinners. (Hebrew 7:26).

4. Joseph told his family he would rule over them and he was ridiculed for that. The Lord Jesus came as the promised Messiah and was nailed to the cross.

5. Joseph was sent by his father to find the brethren. Jesus was sent to his brethren, the house of Israel.

6. Joseph was hated by his brethren for no cause. Jesus was hated by his brethren without cause (John 15:25).

CHAPTER 1: A HISTORY OF ISRAEL

Joseph was sold into slavery by his brothers. A caravan of Ishmaelites and Midianites passed by, traveling together in numbers for safety. Joseph was to rise as a great leader in Egypt, the country he was taken to. It would be a fulfillment of his sun and moon and star dream.

After two years Pharaoh dreamed a double dream meaning the same thing. Joseph was called to interpret Pharaoh's dream which foretold seven years of plentiful harvest followed by seven years of severe famine. Historically it is known that the Nile and its overflowings determine if Egypt eats or not. If the river rises to only twelve cubits a famine is the result. At fourteen cubits it produces a general rejoicing; fifteen, perfect security; and sixteen, all the luxuries of life. When the Nile rises to eighteen cubits it prevents the sowing of the land, and produces a famine just as though it did not overflow its banks.[6]

Joseph correctly interpreted Pharaoh's dreams and at the same time suggested what Pharaoh should do to save Egypt and the world. He laid out a detailed plan to stockpile grain for seven years by the "meery": or fifth part as the land, *"brought forth by handfuls."* (Genesis 41:47). Pharaoh saw that the Spirit of God was endued in Joseph and he was qualified by God for the work so Joseph was made ruler of Egypt second only to Pharaoh.

Joseph was given broad authority and a wife who was a heathen. This parallels Christ who is calling a Gentile bride out of the world which is the Church. Joseph had two sons, Manasseh and Ephraim. The famine thus begins and spreads worldwide. It got severe enough that it forced Jacob to send ten of his sons to Egypt to buy food. He had heard that there was food to be bought in Egypt, and he had faith and acted upon it. When Joseph saw his brothers he did not reveal himself to them nor did they recognize their brother. Only when Joseph demanded them to return with Benjamin, the youngest, did Joseph reveal himself, and told his brothers to bring their father to Egypt.

When Pharaoh finds out that these are the brethren of Joseph, and his father is alive, he extends an invitation for all to come and settle in Egypt. The province of Goshen, the most eastern of Lower Egypt, was to be reserved for Jacob and his family.

> *"And thou shalt dwell in the Land of Goshen, and thou shalt be near unto me, thou, and thy children, and thy children's children, and thy flocks, and thy flocks, and all that thou hast:"* (Genesis 45:10)

Jacob packs up and heads to Beer-Sheba to enquire of God for confirmation and approval, and it is on the way from Hebron to

CHAPTER 1: A HISTORY OF ISRAEL

Egypt. God does appear to him in visions of the night and says:

> *"I am God, the God of thy Father, fear not to go down into Egypt: for I will make of thee a great nation."* (Genesis 46:3)

God will fulfill His covenant in Egypt with Jacob, by making Israel a great nation there. Jacob may have been apprehensive to go to Egypt when God told Abraham to leave Egypt and for Isaac not to go there. The recollection of a prophecy about Egypt and God's people may also have given him pause:

> *"Know of a surety that thy seed shall be a stranger in a land that is not theirs, and shall serve them; and they shall afflict them four hundred years."* (Genesis 15:13)

But Jacob must have known the end of that promise, that "afterward shall they come out with great substance." (Genesis 15:14b). Jacob will be living in Egypt, and he is being carried there now, as a man of faith as the just will live by faith. So, Jacob is in Egypt with his family and including Joseph and his family makes up seventy souls. But if the nine still surviving wives of Jacob's sons are added to the sixty-six, there are a total of seventy-five souls (Acts 7:14).

As Jacob lay upon his deathbed approximately seventeen years after arriving in Goshen, he blesses his sons. It is significant that in the blessing to the son Judah, that we have the line from which the Lord Jesus Christ came from. The prophecy of the seed of the woman, the Lord Jesus Christ, was first given in Genesis 3:15. The seed of the woman Jesus Christ, is the one that bruises the head of Satan and gets the victory. This was confirmed to Abraham, Isaac, and to Jacob, and now to Judah. In Genesis 49:10 it reads:

> "The sceptre shall not depart from Judah, nor a lawgiver from between his feet, until Shiloh come; and unto him shall the gathering of the people be."

An important part of the prophecy is "until Shiloh come." Shiloh is the ruler, and means rest and tranquility, and Christ brings rest. Jesus told the Jews, "come unto me, all ye that labour and are heavy laden, and I will give you rest." (Matthew 12:28) Jesus was telling the Jews that he was Shiloh, and Shiloh or the ruler had come. This ties in with the argument that the Jews even today have with the word scepter. The word scepter is the Hebrew, shebet, which is a rod, and their meaning of it states, "afflictions shall not depart from the Jews till the Messiah comes;" to which they say they are still under affliction, therefore, the Messiah is not come.[7]

The sceptor would not depart from Judah, the King of Israel and his authority will last forever. Judah survived intact until the

CHAPTER 1: A HISTORY OF ISRAEL

Messiah, the Lord Jesus Christ, came to earth, but now is indistinguishable among all Jews.

After blessing his sons, *"all these are the twelve tribes of Israel:"* (Genesis 49:28a), and charging them to bury him where Abraham, Sarah, Isaac and Rebekah and Leah are in rest, Jacob "gathered up his feet into the bed, and yielded up the ghost, and was gathered unto his people." (Genesis 49:33).

We have seen the life of the progenitor patriarchs and the foundation of the nation of Israel in Abraham, Isaac, and Jacob. In strength of mind Abraham seems to have loomed larger than the son, Isaac, and his son Jacob. Jacob had grown from his early times as a sly supplanter into a spiritual leader of the family. God favored all three of the patriarchs and fashioned a nation that would be his light to the nations and produce the Saviour of the human race. These men are our examples of early stages of errors and mistakes in life and surrendering to God to become great pillars of the faith.

So the patriarchs were buried together in the hope of that blessed resurrection according to the promise of God.

> *"These died in faith, not having received the promises, but having seen them afar off,..."* (Hebrews 11:13a)

After the death of Jacob the brothers go to Joseph and fall down before him to pray for his forgiveness. Joseph tells them to have no fear as long as he is alive for he will care for them.

> *"But as for you, ye thought evil against me; but God meant it unto good,..."* (Genesis 50:20a)

God had all this under his control. As Joseph lay dying he gave this testimony of his faith in God.

> *"By faith Joseph, when he died, made mention of the departing of the children of Israel; and gave commandment concerning his bones."* (Hebrews 11:22)

Joseph wanted to be removed from Egypt and buried among the fathers, to be raised to heaven at the resurrection, from the eternal possession that would be the land of Canaan.

At this point in their history, Israel is now into their serving 400 years in Egypt. In Genesis 15:13 it says:

> *"And they shall afflict them four hundred years;" in a land that is not theirs, which in fact was Egypt. For their afflicting God's people who served them, the Egyptians, "will I judge:"* (Genesis 15:16)

> *"And the children of Israel were fruitful and increased abundantly, and multiplied, and waxed exceeding mighty and the land was filled with them."* (Exodus 1:7)

CHAPTER 1: A HISTORY OF ISRAEL

Here we see the partial fulfillment of the covenant God had made with Abraham in Genesis 12:2 where he would multiply and make Israel a great nation. God restates the promise in a vision to Jacob in Genesis 46:3, "For I will there make of thee a great nation:" And God did multiply them to the alarm of the Egyptians, which led to greater afflictions and burdens put on the Israelites. The first effort to exterminate the Jews came about when the King of Egypt ordered the death of the Hebrew male babies when they were born. If this had succeeded the Jewish nation would have shortly been destroyed. The midwives obeyed God and not Pharaoh.

Moses

God begins the preparation of a deliverer for Israel who are being ruthlessly oppressed.

> *"And Amram took him Jocebed his father sister to wed; and she bore him Aaron and Moses:"* (Exodus 6:20)

The population of the Israelites had been growing in Egypt under the oppression of the Pharaohs. The people were the slaves of the Egyptians. Since Moses had been taken and raised as Pharaoh's oldest daughter's first-born son, he would have been the next Pharaoh if Rameses II and the queen had remained childless. Moses was taught by the Egyptians.

> *"And Moses was learned in all the wisdom of the Egyptians, and was mighty in words and in deeds."* (Acts 7:22)

As Moses went walking he saw a Hebrew, whom he felt akin to, being beaten by a slave driver, so Moses killed the Egyptian and it was discovered the next day. Moses fled to Midian. For the next forty years God prepares Moses as deliverer of the Israelites. Things were not going so good in Egypt for Israel.

> *"And their cry came up unto God by reason of their bondage. And God heard their groaning, and God remembered his covenant with Abraham, with Isaac, and with Jacob."* (Exodus 2: 23b, 24)

God heard from heaven the cries of his chosen people. He was going to deliver them and God through Moses was going to do this. He was going to do this because of the covenant made with Abraham, Isaac, and Jacob. The Israelites were in a hopeless state and God was going to extend his mercy to them. It is the same for us who had nothing within us that warranted salvation or any merit on our own. The Lord saves us from our helpless state without a cause. It was only because we cannot save ourselves that God gave his only begotten son Jesus to die for our sins. We are saved by that grace.

God saw Israel for what it was, a people of sinners, in bondage and helpless. He had a plan for Israel and was going to use Moses to demonstrate his power and defeat Pharaoh from destroying his people.

The Call of Moses

The first forty years of the life of Moses were spent in the Court of Pharaoh. He has just completed another forty years of his preparation in the land of Midian. In this desert area God has prepared Moses for the great work of delivering Israel from bondage.

> "And the Angel of the Lord appeared unto him in a flame of fire out of the midst of a bush:" (Exodus 3:2a)

Bush is from the Hebrew, Seneh, from which in a flame the Lord appeared to Moses. This appearance or theophany, not a created angel, for He is called Jehovah, with all the attributes of the Godhead fully. He is manifested as an Angel in whom was the name of God, the fullness of the Godhead, (Colossians 2:9), the messenger of the Covenant. This is Jesus Christ, leader, redeemer, and Saviour. For this was the same Jehovah that Hagar was convinced appeared to her in the wilderness, *"and she called the name of the Lord that spoke unto her, Thou God seest me:"* (Genesis 16:13).

All these things cannot be spoken of any human or created being, for the knowledge, works, etc., attributed to this person are such as belong to God; and as in all these cases there is a most evident personal appearance, Jesus Christ alone can be meant; for of God the Father it has ever been true that no man hath at any time seen his shape, nor has he ever limited himself to any definable personal appearance.[8]

> *"And he looked, and behold, the bush burned with fire, and the bush was not consumed."* (Exodus 3:2b)

We can say that Israel as a nation is a nation that has travailed in the fire of adversity, but was not consumed. Such is the protection of the nation by God himself. As Christians we are walking through the fire but also are not consumed for God is in our midst. God is preserving the bush, he is preserving the nation of Israel and he is preserving his saints and his church. Our Lord and his burning message to the word should cause unbelievers of the world to turn away from their sin and look to Jesus Christ. The miracles of Israel, the nation, and the church with believers through the centuries of having not been consumed ought to be witness to God and His truth.

> *"God called unto him out of the midst of the bush, and said, Moses, Moses. And he said, Here am I."* (Exodus 3:4)

God told Moses that he had heard the cries of affliction from his people and that he was

CHAPTER 1: A HISTORY OF ISRAEL

going to deliver them out of bondage and bring them to a land flowing with milk and honey. It was a land, *"of brooks of water, of fountains and depths that spring out of valleys and hills; a land of wheat, and barley, and vines, and fig trees, and pomegranates; a land of oil olive, and honey;"* (Deuteronomy 8: 7,8).

God is sending Moses back to Egypt to deliver his people. Moses was ready to do God's work, but was reluctant that God wanted to accomplish the task that was beyond Moses' own power. It was going to take supernatural means for the Israelites to escape their oppressors. *"When thou hast brought forth the people out of Egypt, ye shall serve God upon this mountain."* (Exodus 3:12) Moses and all Israel will come to Mount Sinai on their way to the Promised Land. The very spot that Moses received his command from God Israel will receive their commandments also.

Moses returns to Egypt to do all the wonders before Pharaoh, *"but I will harden his heart, that he will not let the people go."* (Exodus 4:21b).

God is taking all the power and glory for what he will do in Egypt to free his people. He will necessarily control Pharaoh's heart in order to fully implement his signs to all the people that he is God and not the Egyptian idols that have any power whatsoever. God will withhold graces of a softened heart, of an enlightened heart, and an open heart to the call of God in Pharaoh. Pharaoh's heart will be presumptuous, tough, stiff, and stubborn when dealing with Moses and the Israelites. By being continuously stubborn, bold, haughty and cruel, Pharaoh rushes onward to his own destruction. In each episode of Pharaoh's haughtiness, God had the opportunity to manifest his power by multiplying signs and miracles for the Egyptian and Israelite people to see the omnipotence and justice of God. It will have the effect of strengthening the faith of the Israelites in their God, and shake the faith of Egyptians in their gods. It was therefore necessary that the divine method of hardening of the heart of Pharaoh be enacted in order for the actions against the Egyptian gods be carried out in divine order. This would not have occurred if Pharaoh immediately agreed to let the Israelites go. The hardening process did not negate to God the execution of justice. The opposite was true. Pharaoh's own pride and presumption was self-enhanced by only the withholding of enlightening grace by God. God did not have to lead Pharaoh into such offenses as Pharaoh was capable of, but merely withdrew Pharaoh's ability to attain God's graces at every stage of his choice for the Israelites freedom following each plague. Pharaoh had every opportunity to let Israel go, and God was giving him those opportunities,

CHAPTER 1: A HISTORY OF ISRAEL

but Pharaoh was a godless man. God was being fair to Pharaoh and he rebuffed God at every turn. The hearts of the Egyptians were not to be hardened, but by each plague the possibility of salvation for each soul was to be extended as an escape from their sinning state. The justice and sovereignty of God is magnified not by the sending of plagues but by the exposure of the ineptness of one's gods, and idols revealed as inferior compared to an omnipotent God.

The first attempt of Moses to get Pharaoh to let the people of Israel go was met by derision as he said, *"who is the LORD,....I know not the LORD, neither will I let Israel go."* (Exodus 5:2) Pharaoh, as did all of Egypt, knew not the God of Israel, the great Jehovah. However, that was about the change. For the present, Pharaoh only increased the workload for the Israelites. This dismayed the Israelites and increased their fear of the Egyptians. God was about the plague Egypt and make Himself known.

> *"And the Egyptians shall know that I am the Lord, when I stretch forth mine hand upon Egypt, and bring out the children of Israel from among them."*
> (Exodus 7:6)

The plagues that the Lord brought upon Egypt were ten, and they were organized and meaningful as they were directed against the gods of Egypt. The plagues represented the battle against the power in the Egyptian religions as Satanic.

> *"Now as Jannes and Jambres withstood Moses, so do these also resist the truth; men of corrupt minds, reprobate concerning the faith."* (2 Timothy 3:8)

Plague number one was the waters of Egypt turned into blood. (Exodus 7:19-25).

> *"The Egyptians shall loathe to drink of the water of the river."* (Exodus 7:18)

The first of ten plagues, all of which will occur within a month's span, affected the very sweet tasting and beloved thirst quenching waters of the Nile. When a person drinks of the Nile's waters for the first time, "he can scarcely be persuaded that it is not a water prepared by art."[9]

The plague of blood extended to all Egyptian waterways and even the personal filtration systems throughout the land. This plague was against the main object of Egyptian idolatry, the Nile. It was directed toward the fertility gods and Osiris who is only one of the main gods of the country.

The second plague is of frogs (Exodus 8:1-15) which covered the whole land. The animals sprang from the river Nile and invaded every nook and cranny of every house. They covered everything so much so that Pharaoh

CHAPTER 1: A HISTORY OF ISRAEL

wanted Moses to ask the Lord to take away the frogs so the people could go. When Pharaoh saw that the plague of frogs was stayed he hardened his heart and would not let the people go. This plague was directed at Heka, the frog-headed goddess whose beautiful temple was in Memphis. The frog was sacred to the Egyptians.

The third plague (Exodus 8:16-20) was of lice which all the dust became lice in the people and in all the beasts of the land. The Egyptians worshipped the earth-god Geb, which this plague represented. The dust which was sacred to Geb was now despised by the Egyptians. This caused great discomfort, especially to their priests who had to keep their bodies clean shaven so as to not have the lice settle upon them. The Egyptian sorceries were not able to copycat this plague. The self-realization was starting to set in that the God who was bringing the plague was far superior to their own gods.

Pharaoh's hardness of heart led to the fourth plague, (Exodus 8:20-32), the plague of flies. God now begins his division between His people and the Egyptians.

> *"And I will put a division between my people and thy people: Tomorrow shall this sign be."* (Exodus 8:23)

Some have speculated, namely Bochart, that the fly referred to the dog-fly. The Egyptians highly venerated dogs and worshipped Anubis in the form of a dog. The land of Egypt was inundated by swarms of flies and the land was corrupted.

"He sent divers sorts of flies around them, which devoured them. (Psalm 78:45)

The Egyptians had deities to supposedly protect them from all kinds of flying insects. Many were possibly stung to death by flying venomous insects. McGee attributes the flies to include the sacred scarab or beetle, which the Egyptians were known to produce in gold and line the tombs of Egypt with. They were sacred to and represented the Egyptian sun god Ra. Now their sacred beetle was a curse to them. It was also becoming clear to all that since Goshen, where the Israelites were, would not be affected by the plagues from here on out, that the judgment was upon them only.

The pressure upon Pharaoh is turned up with the fifth plague unleashed on Egypt. This is the plague of murrain which falls on all the Egyptian cattle, horses, asses, camels, oxen, and upon the sheep. The Hebrew word for murrain is "deber", a pestilence, a destroying pestilence. The particular disease strain in the fifth plague is not known, but murrains are very serious and deadly outbreaks that cause

CHAPTER 1: A HISTORY OF ISRAEL

sudden and widespread death of cattle and other animals.

This serious plague was against Apis and Hathor, the gods of the sacred bull and cow. The large temple built in Memphis was for the worship of the black bull Apis.

The sixth plague (Exodus (9:8-17) was the plague of boils. This was aimed at the Egyptian gods of health and disease. One was Sekhmet the goddess of epidemics. The others, Sunu, Serapis, and Imhotep, were gods of healing. The Pharaoh's magicians also were afflicted with the intense boils so that they could not stand against Moses. Just one boil is enough to cause a fever in the body. To be covered in a multitude of boils was excruciating. Boils with blains meant that they protruded outward of the body and were blistered and swelled pustules which caused a severe agony. God was getting very severe and personal now in the plagues. He let it be known to Pharaoh that he was the cause of his people's suffering for he had afflicted God's people. God was not finished convincing Pharaoh and the Egyptians that he is mighty and the only true God.

God then warned that any cattle that were left alive to the Egyptians should be sheltered against the grievous hail about to fall. This seventh plague of hail was brought against Nut or Shu, the goddess of the sky and atmosphere. It also came against Isis and Set, the agricultural gods.

The hail, which was unlike any before it, "so there was hail, and fire mingled with the hail, very grievous, such as there was none like it in all the Land of Egypt since it became a nation." The men and cattle left in the fields were destroyed, as well as all the crops and trees left broken. *"Where the children of Israel were, was there no hail."* (Exodus 9:26). The flax, used for production of linen, and the barley were rendered smitten. The wheat and rye were not smitten in the hail and will figure in the next plague.

Pharaoh did not like all the thunderings and the hail but his hardened heart would not give in to God. The eighth plague of swarms and swarms of locusts were unleased against mainly Serapis, the protecting deity against Locusts. The Gods of Nut, Osiris, and Set were also attacked in this plague. *"And the Lord brought an east wind upon the land all that day, and all that night; and when it was morning, the east wind brought the locusts."* (Exodus 10:13) These locusts were hungry and devoured everything in their path. *"They did eat every herb of the land, and all the fruit of the trees which the hail had left: and there remained not any green thing in the trees, or*

CHAPTER 1: A HISTORY OF ISRAEL

in the herbs of the field, through all the land of Egypt." (Exodus 10:15)

After the Lord had hardened Pharaoh's heart again, the ninth plague of thick darkness was sent over the land of Egypt for three days. It was so thick and dark no one could see another person, nor get up out of their place for fear of crashing into something and getting lost. Nothing could give its light. The Egyptians were prisoners in their darkness. Every human being is held captive in their own darkness before coming to the light of salvation in the Lord Jesus Christ. In this darkness,

"he cast upon them the fierceness of his anger, wrath, and indignation, and trouble, by sending evil angels among them." (Psalm 78:49)

It was truly a scary time. In the absence of light the darkness to the Egyptians would mean death, judgment, and hopelessness.

All of this combined to come against the main Egyptian god of the sun, Ra. The Sun god was symbolized by Pharaoh himself. In a lesser degree the plague of darkness was leveled against the sun gods of Amonre, Atem, Atum, and Horus. It was also aimed at Thoth, the Egyptian moon god.

God knew that Pharaoh would not let the Israelites go after the first nine terrible plagues, and that it would take one night to slay all the first-born, both man and beast, throughout Egypt. He would not give up his sin, his fame, and his power, even in a death match with the Almighty God. Pharaoh's hardening of himself from the fear of God has now brought about his and his country's destruction. We each need to examine our own frail selves, our common behavior of relenting under God's judgments, but hardening our hearts when God removes the judgments. We indeed reap what we sow.

The Freeing of Israel

The tenth and final plague was to be a collective judgment on all Egypt and their ungodly idolatry. The firstborn, according to Egyptian religion belonged to the gods of Egypt. God was going to take from the Egyptian gods that which was dedicated to them. God wanted all the Egyptians to know who he is. He was showing Pharaoh that he was God. At the same time God was bringing his people to a place where they would acknowledge him as their God.

The freeing of Israel entailed the first nine plagues upon Egypt, the Tenth and most crushing plague, the hand of God in power, and the Passover. There was yet one plague more upon Pharaoh that God was giving to bring about. Afterwards, God said, The

CHAPTER 1: A HISTORY OF ISRAEL

Israelites will be let go. According to the preparation for departure God would give the Israelite people favor in the sight of the Egyptians.

> "But every woman shall borrow of her neighbor, and of her that sojourneth in her house, jewels of silver, and jewels of gold;...and ye shall spoil the Egyptians." (Exodus 3:22)

The Egyptians were to compensate the Israelite services rendered and this would amount of a spoil of an enemy so as to not be leaving empty. It is understood that a slave could not accumulate any wealth or property, thus God ensures his people the reparations that extended back to Joseph's time. Egypt owed its own survival and opulence to the Israelites and thus to God. The Israelites had been abused, enslaved, forced to build fortresses and treasure cities for no compensation. They had to abide as their male infants were murdered daily. They were to take gold and silver and clothing with them for their journey. They had to spoil the Egyptians for what had been done to them and taken from them. This was the favor of God and the blessing upon his people. This is an injustice which God saw to make right.

> "Moreover the man Moses was very great in the land of Egypt, in the sight of Pharaoh's servants, and in the sight of the people." (Exodus 12:3)

This is in fulfillment of God's promise to Moses to be with him in bringing his people out of Egypt. It was God who made Moses great in Egypt and make himself known to the Egyptians.

> *"All my wonders which I will do in the midst thereof: after that he will let you go."* (Exodus 3:20).

Moses told the people that the Lord will go out at midnight into the midst of Egypt.

> *"And all the first-born in the land of Egypt shall die,"* (Exodus 11:5a)

The blood of the Egyptians was going to be shed, but the blood of lambs which portrayed the Lord Jesus Christ, was to put a difference between the Egyptians and the Israelites.

The Institution of the Passover

God is instituting the first month of the year the month of Abib which corresponds to our Western March in which the Israelites would point out to their posterity what month and what day they would celebrate the Passover.

On the tenth day of the first month ABIB, in the original Passover they would take a lamb for a house. The twelve tribes were divided into families, the families into houses, and the houses would be further divided into persons.

Now there has been some controversy in the Church by some correctors over the original word (Shaal) for borrow in the twenty-second verse. The same Shaal is used in Exodus 11:1-3 and in Exodus 11:33-36. The same word Shaal used in Exodus 11: 33-36 is translated as borrowed and lent. This is also true in Exodus 12:35-36. The modernists, Bible correctors, and religionists contort the word in all manner so as to avoid the use in context.

Clarke calls borrow a very exceptionable term.[10] He also states, this is certainly not a very correct translation: the original word, shaal, signifies simply to ask, request, demand, require, inquire, etc.; but it does not signify to borrow in the proper sense of that word.[11]

However, in God's sense of the word it has everything to do with borrowing. This will be the first instance where wealth is to be bestowed upon the Israelites. God promised this in his prophecy to Abraham concerning the nation of Israel.

> *"And also that nation, whom they shall serve, will I judge: and afterward shall they come out with great substance."* (Genesis 15:14)

So, it is a fact that all the great substance that God gave to the Israelites was substantial and it was necessarily borrowed in the sense it was "on loan." As it turned out Israel lost it all and Egypt got back some of what was "borrowed."

> "So Shishak King of Egypt came up against Jerusalem, and took away the treasures of the house of the LORD, and the treasures of the king's house; he took all: he carried away also the shields of gold which Solomon had made." (11 Chronicles 12:9)

Then there is the definition for Shaal in the Complete Word Study Dictionary, inspired by Dr. Spiros Zodhiates. They state on page 1085, very rarely, the term (Shaal) could refer to borrowing or lending. But this is certainly not the meaning when the people of Israel asked goods from the Egyptians they plundered.

Granted, the main rendering of the word Shaal is "ask" and that meaning is given for it in the Bible 88 times. It is also used as "enquire" some 22 times. It can be given a meaning of "to ask as a loan, as found in the "Analytical Hebrew and Chaldee Lexicon." In versus 18-22 of Exodus God gives Moses the instructions on how he would deal with Pharaoh. At first God had Moses present Pharaoh with the idea of a three day journey into the wilderness to sacrifice and worship God. It was traditional in those areas of the

Middle East that the people would put on their best jewelry for the occasion. So at first all of the people and all of the Egyptians were to understand that this was only a three day foray and as such were very willing to lend their best jewels to the Israelites. God had every intention of bringing his people out of Egypt and by giving the Israelites favor in the eyes of the Egyptians, *"ye shall spoil the Egyptians."* Exodus 3:22). It is to be remembered that according to custom the borrowed articles willingly given were considered gifts.

This incident fulfilled three things: It was the way that God spoiled the Egyptians in judgment; the Israelites were given reparations for centuries of slavery; and God fulfilled his prophecy to Abraham in Genesis 15:14.

The same is true today as given by God in Deuteronomy 15: 13-15, known as the backsheesh.

> *"And when thou sendest him (a servant) out free from thee, thou shalt not let him go away empty: and thou shalt remember that thou wast a bondman in the Land of Egypt, and the Lord they God redeemed thee: therefore I command thee this thing today."* (Deuteronomy 15: 13, 15)

The lamb would have to be without blemish and kept until it was killed on the fourteenth day of the month. The Rabbis through the years have dictated that there were fifty blemishes that made a lamb improper: five in the ear, three in the eyelid, eight in the eye, three in the nose, six in the mouth, and on and on. [10]

These four days before the killing of the lamb were to be for examining the Passover lambs for any blemish. It must be a perfect lamb. On the fourteenth day of the month they were to kill the lamb, each house of the Israelites were to do this. The blood of the lambs was to be caught in basins and then each household would take hyssop branches and apply the blood to door posts and lintel of the door. Then they were to take the flesh of the lamb and roast it and eat it until there was nothing left by morning.

There were some things unique to this first Passover that were not carried over afterwards. 1) They ate the lamb in their houses which were in Goshen. 2) The taking of the lamb on the tenth day of the month. It would be taken on the day before Passover subsequently. 3) The application of the blood on the doorposts and lintels of the houses. 4) The eating of the Passover lamb in haste.

The Spiritual Side of Passover

"For even Christ our Passover is sacrificed for us." (1 Corinthians 5:7)

CHAPTER 1: A HISTORY OF ISRAEL

To the Israelites in Egypt the Passover was a feast given to them by God as a deliverance from their slavery and a beginning for them to journey to the Promised land. What is the Passover a picture of for Christians? As Paul wrote in 1 Corinthians 5:7, Christ is our Passover Lamb who was sacrificed for us. Just as the Israelites were saved from death by the blood on the doorposts, sinners are saved by the blood of Christ that was shed on Calvary's cross. The Lord Jesus Christ is the most important part in Passover. In its application the Passover lamb looked forward to Christ's sacrifice on the cross. We are saved:

> *"With the precious blood of Christ, as of a lamb without blemish and without spot:"* (1 Peter 1:19)

> *"He is brought as a lamb to the slaughter, and as a sheep before her shearers,"* (Isaiah 53:7)

John the Baptist said of Christ,

> *"Behold the Lamb of God, which taketh away the sin of the world."* (John 1:29)

Jesus Christ is the Lamb of God who was without blemish, sinless and holy. He was killed and shed his blood at the very time of the Passover for the Jews which was the perfect fulfillment of God's word. The blood of Christ is applied to our hearts when we believe by faith which saves us from death and hell.

> *"Verily, verily, I say unto you, he that hearth my word, and believeth on him that sent me, hath everlasting life,"* (John 5:24a)

Just as pending death awaited firstborn children and animals in Egypt who did not obey the Lord's directions, death awaits those who reject Christ. To escape in Egypt blood had to be applied to the doorposts. It was either lamb's blood or else the blood of the firstborn. Someone or something had to die to escape death. Christ can be obeyed and accepted as our substitute for our sin who bore our punishment to satisfy God's justice against sin. Otherwise we would bear our own punishment for all eternity in a burning hell. When judgment and punishment for sin comes, our choice is on whom will this fall. It could come down on us individually or if we believe on Jesus Christ it will be on the Lamb of God, God's holy, sinless sacrifice.

> *"Who his own self bear our sins in his own body on the tree, that we, being dead to sins, should live unto righteousness:"* (1 Peter 2:24)

The Passover Lamb was God's way of making an escape for the Israelites. They were to be spared the certain death of each firstborn child and the entire nation of Israel was to be redeemed from the bondage of slavery in Egypt. God's provision for Israel was realized when the Passover's blood of the lamb was applied to the doors of the houses of the Israelites. God's provision of eternal life will do none of us any good unless the Blood of the Lamb of God is applied to the door of the heart by the hyssop of faith in Christ.

Death of Firstborn

The institution of the Passover Feast was to be a memorial to the deliverance of Israel from the bondage of Egypt.

> *"For I will pass through the Land of Egypt this night."* (Exodus 12:12a)

> *"I am the Lord." (Exodus 12:12b)*

> *"And when I see the blood, I will pass over you."* (Exodus 12:13)

The blood that was to be applied from the slain lambs to the doorposts of all the houses was a sign to the Lord that those in the house were safe from this last plague. The plague was not to be upon those who had the blood applied.

> *"For the Lord will pass through to smite the Egyptians; and when he seeth the blood upon the lintel, and on the two side posts, the Lord will pass over the door,"* (Exodus 12:23)

The Israelites were to keep this service when they came into their land which the Lord was giving them, to tell their generations of the night passed over their houses and smote the Egyptians.

The Egyptians slept that night even though nine terrible plagues had come and gone. Unexpectantly, as they lay sleeping, the Lord smote all the firstborn in the land of Egypt. This plague was executed as a judgment on all of the Egyptian gods, including Pharaoh himself. After killing the sons of Israel, now the firstborn sons of Egypt are killed. This was also a plague against Isis, the protector of children, and against Ptah, the God of Life.

The Israelites escaped this plague also, as the blood was applied. The Egyptians could have escaped by applied blood but chose to go to sleep in unbelief instead. Pharaoh and his people finally woke up and a great cry went up all over Egypt as every Egyptian household had at least one death.

Deliverance

The amount of loss, horror, and distress felt by the Egyptians was too much for Pharaoh. The people themselves were in such a state of shock and greatly feared the God of Israel to the point they all felt that they were going to die. They wanted the Israelites to go and as soon as possible.

The Israelites took unleavened bread and bowls, their clothing, silver and gold, and

CHAPTER 1: A HISTORY OF ISRAEL

journeyed to Succoth. The men, women, children, Levites, their wives and children, and mixed multitude that made up the nation of Israel leaving Egypt would amount to upwards of three million people. Just the sheer numbers would necessarily have scared Moses but for the fact that he had God's approval and provision for his Divine Mission.

God was going to lead Moses back to Mt. Sinai/Mt. Horeb where he commissioned Moses to free Israel from Egypt. God was going to fashion a nation out of a disorganized mass by giving them laws by which to obey. *"When thou hast brought forth the people out of Egypt, ye shall serve God upon this mountain."* (Exodus 3:12b) The sign God gives Moses came out of the burning bush that through Moses he would deliver Israel and through Moses would give his law upon their return.

As Israel approached the Red Sea, the Egyptians were in hot pursuit. But God, as he had promised, would protect Israel all during the night by the pillar of the cloud and the Angel of God. This separated the two camps as the Sea parted. The Israelites made their way through the waters on dry ground, "the waters were a wall unto them on their right hand and on their left." (Exodus 14:22). The Egyptians went right in after them but the Lord looked, "through the pillar of fire of the cloud, and troubled the host of the Egyptians." (Exodus 14:24). This caused the destruction of the chariots of the Egyptians, and they turned to flee. But the Lord made the water to crash down over the chariots, and the horsemen, and all the host of Pharaoh were destroyed. "There remained not so much as one of them: (Exodus 14:28b) As the Lord redeemed the Israelites that day, the Lord does the same for us. There is no redemption but for the work of the Lord. A miracle took place to save the Israelites from destruction, as does a miracle take place in our hearts to save us from destruction. Salvation is of the Lord.

God had performed two great miracles for Israel: the deliverance from slavery in Egypt, and delivering Israel to safety across the Red Sea and destroying the pursuing Egyptians. It is the Lord's deliverance and redemption. It is his salvation and when we are saved we are joined to Christ through the Holy Spirit.

> *"For by one Spirit are we all baptized into one body, whether we be Jews or Gentiles, whether he be bond or free; and have been all made to drink into one Spirit."*
> (1 Corinthians 12:13)

God had delivered on his only promise to Abraham concerning the nation Israel.

> *"And also that nation, whom they shall serve, will I judge: and afterward shall they*

come out with great substance." (Genesis 15:14)

Abrahamic Covenant Revisited

It would be worthwhile to study again the covenant made by God to Abraham and see how it is progressing now that Israel has escaped from Egypt. As is known Egypt is a type of the world and having crossed over the Red Sea, Israel is now dependent upon God for their continued existence.

With the covenant comes the continuance of the promises of a land, a nation, a people, etc. The original giving of the covenant appeared in Genesis 12:1-3.

> *1."Now the Lord had said unto Abram, get thee out of thy country, and from thy kindred and from thy father's house, unto a land that I will shew thee:*
>
> *2. And I will make of thee a great nation, and I will bless thee, and make thy name great; and thou shalt be a blessing.*
>
> *3. And I will bless them that bless thee, and curse him that curseth thee: and in thee shall all families of the earth be blessed."*

As Israel proceeds through the wilderness, Moses is leading them to the land promised by God. They will be planted in that land by God and conditionally and permanently given that land forever. Any failure by Israel will require discipline but will not cancel the covenant. The question arises about the Abrahamic and by extension, The Davidic covenants being conditional or unconditional as established by God. When God tells Abraham to leave his country, his kindred, and his father's house, and he will shew him a land, make him a great nation, make his name great and a blessing, does that put a condition on God's unconditional covenant?

Both Dr. Dwight Pentecost and Dr. John F. Walvoord, who both take the unconditional character of the covenant, believe "there is a condition to be fulfilled by Abraham between the promise of God to him in Ur and the actual establishment of the covenant." [13]

They say that the promise made to Abraham depended on his act and acts of obedience and that whether God would institute a covenant with him depended on Abraham leaving his country. The obedience in completion to the establishment of the covenant is evidence in Genesis 22:18 with the offering of Isaac in sacrifice.

As proof Dr. Walvoord concludes that no further revelation from God is given to Abraham until after the death of Abraham's father, Terah. Therefore, when Abraham obeyed, no further continued obedience was

CHAPTER 1: A HISTORY OF ISRAEL

needed to institute the covenant but for the promise of God who promised it.

There are those who insist that Abraham's continued obedience was necessary to the fulfillment of the covenant. These would be the amillennialists. For all of the combined obedience of Abraham to be counted as being necessary for the establishment of the covenant would have led to the separation from Lot to be the convenant's establishment. Abraham's shifting fulfillment of the condition of obedience from Genesis 11:31 to 22:16 would definitely play into the hands of the amillennialists. This line of reasoning is against the establishment of an unconditional covenant. Not one act of obedience on the part of Abraham can be accepted as a condition for the Abrahamic Covenant.

Mason conjectures that there is a basic hermeneutical understanding as a solution. That is the

> "recognition that the sequence of the oft-repeated word "and" merely connects the clauses of Genesis 12:1 with those of 12:2 and 12:3" [14]

In Genesis 12:1-3 God did not predicate his covenant with Abraham on his obedience to leave Ur, his kindred and father's house. Before Abraham left Ur God had already pre-announced his covenant to Abraham. It was not a, you do this then I will do that kind of deal. God gave Abraham those commands and knew he would obey those commands, thus the obedience to those commands was not the basis of the unconditional covenant. These are sequential events that followed naturally as God implemented his covenant. The proper interpretation of the "ands" is that they are conjunctions, making one whole the spoken related statements. The Omniscient God is unfolding foretold events. It was the almighty's purpose to give the unconditional covenant through Abraham to his descendants, to the nation of Israel and to the world. It will ultimately be fulfilled through Abraham's seed, The Lord Jesus Christ.

To complete the thought on obedience conditioning the covenant it must be stated that the covenant was unconditionally given to Abraham, a person God knew would obey him because Abraham believed God and loved God.

> *"Seeing that Abraham shall surely become a great and mighty nation, and all the nations of the earth shall be blessed in him?"* (Genesis 18:18).

> *"For because thou hast done this thing, and hast not withheld thy son,...and in thy seed shall all the nations of the earth be blessed; because thou hast obeyed my voice."* (Genesis 22:16, 18)

God is declaring that the obedience of Abraham is complete now that Abraham was willing to sacrifice his only son. God was still dealing with Abraham's obedience but his continuous obedience was not an aspect of the covenant's institution by God. God knew of the willingness of Abraham to obey him, but at what point can we say that Abraham's obedience was sufficient enough for God to establish his covenant? But we know that the institution of the unconditional covenant with Abraham was long before he obeyed God in Genesis 22.

Unconditional or Conditional Covenants

A covenant is a solemn pronouncement of God by which he establishes a relationship of responsibility between himself and a man or group of mankind.[15]

The messenger or bringer of the covenant is the Lord Jesus Christ.

> *"Behold, I will send my messenger, and he shall prepare the way before me: and the LORD, whom ye seek, shall suddenly come to his temple, even the messenger of the covenant,"* (Malachi 3:1)

> *"To perform the mercy promised to our fathers, and to remember his holy covenant; the oath which he swear to our father Abraham,"* (Luke 1: 72,73)

Covenants are contracts between God and man and result in the promise of blessings to those accepting and are under such agreements and live accordingly to the Lord. In the Old Testament God made covenants with Adam, Noah, Abraham, and his descendants which were the Israelites. The Old Testament Term Covenant is Berith, in the Hebrew. The New Testament Greek, diatheke, is the word covenant and God's covenant is with the Church through the Lord Jesus Christ, the new covenant.

Conditional Covenants

When man is involved in any covenant with God, that part of making a promise is always considered conditional. Therefore, man must be in continuous obedience to what he promised in the covenant or the blessing is voided. God is providing the granted blessings to man dependent on man fulfilling certain conditions contained in the covenant. Any failure on man's part to uphold the conditions will result in discipline or punishment. The Edenic Covenant (Genesis 1:28) and the Mosaic Covenant (Exodus 19:25) are conditional covenants. The establishment of the conditional covenant is dependent upon man accepting the terms of the contract. An example of such is found in Israel's acceptance of the terms in the Mosaic covenant.

CHAPTER 1: A HISTORY OF ISRAEL

> *"Now therefore, if ye will obey my voice indeed, and keep my covenant, then ye shall be a peculiar treasure unto me above all people:" (Exodus 19:5)*
>
> *"And all the people answered together, and said, all that the Lord hath spoken we will do." (Exodus 19:8)*

Unconditional Covenants

The unconditional covenants include the Adamic Covenant, The Noahic Covenant, the Abrahamic Covenant (Genesis 12:1-3), the Land Covenant (Deuteronomy 30:1-10), The Davidic Covenant (2 Samuel 7:10-16), and the New Covenant (Hebrew 8:80, Jeremiah 31: 31-40).

An unconditional covenant is a unilateral covenant and is a sovereign act of God whereby he unconditionally obliges himself to bring to pass definite blessings and conditions for the covenanted people. [16]

These types of covenants were not conditioned to the behavior of man. The result of any behavior that was good was blessed and bad behavior was cursed. Unconditional covenants will not change for any reason or be nullified by human error. God is immutable, and the truth is unconditional. Man serves himself and is unreliably changeable. When God makes a covenant or promise with man, that promise is unconditional and we can believe God to keep that promise. The opposite is unfortunately true for man.

Mosaic Covenant

In the conditional covenant it will be remembered that the condition or conditions of that covenant is what precedes the establishment of the covenant. Once accepted the covenant is then ratified. The distinguishing characteristic between the types of covenants is that when man's failure occurs during the conditional covenant God can void the contract. Unconditional covenants do not depend upon man's obedience. They are firm contracts no matter what and remain unchangeable and inviolate as the character of God himself.

Israel has been led by God to Mount Sinai. There they will be given the covenant of law in moral commandments, social judgments, and religious ordinances.

> *"And Moses went up unto God, and the Lord called unto him out of the mountain, saying, thus shalt thou say to the house of Jacob, and tell the children of Israel:"* (Exodus 19:3)

It is interesting that God reminds the people that he has borne them on eagle's wings, by the grace of God and they have arrived safely at the Mount. Christians are led by God's grace and the just walk by faith. The

CHAPTER 1: A HISTORY OF ISRAEL

Israelites faced with the choice to continue in grace are about to accept the law and commandments. Christians do the same thing today, exchanging grace for law. The people responded to God in Egypt when they employed the blood by faith and listened to God when they marched to the mountain. They were free and obeyed in grace and God brought them unto Himself.

Today, God saves by grace, not by law. Not only revealing the great, good character of God, the law reveals the weakness of man. Works by law do not save, grace gives rest from work. We believe by grace through faith, but the law commands us to do. Law is threatening, pronouncing a curse. Grace pleads urgently, bestowing a blessing. Law is not given as a path of salvation. The purpose then of the law given by God is stated as:

> *"Wherefore then serveth the law? It was added because of transgressions, till the seed should come to whom the promise was made;"* (Galatians 3:19)

The law gives sin the character of being a transgression or an offence against God. Up until the giving of the law sin was not put to the sinner's account, even though the human race was sinning before Moses.

> *"For until the law sin was in the world: but sin is not imputed when there is no law."* (Romans 5:13)

For the believer, imputation is an act of God where he accounts or reckons righteousness to us in Christ, since he has borne our sins in vindication of the law. Christ says he does this, *"If he hath wronged thee, or oweth the ought, put that on mine account."* (Philemon, Verse 18) Jesus says to put his payment up against his account that he has made good to the Father for our transgressions of debt that we owe. By the act of faith we transfer our sins to the Lord Jesus Christ and God credits Christ's righteousness to those, who believe. Imputation is from the Greek, Logizomai "to reckon in," "to charge to one's account."

The law says that all are guilty of sin before God. The law was given for an intervening time until the seed, or Christ should come. The law shut man up or directed him by faith as the only avenue of escape from sins' damnation.

The law was the schoolmaster to bring one to Christ. In Roman times the schoolmaster was a slave in the household who took care of a child or children. The child was raised by the pedagogue, who ruled the child. This was the character of the law until Christ came to justify the believer by faith. Since Christ has come, the believer is not under the pedagogue of the law.

CHAPTER 1: A HISTORY OF ISRAEL

> *"Christ hath redeemed us from the curse of the law, being made a curse for us:"* (Galatians 3:13)

When Moses communicated the idea of a covenant from God to the Israelites he heard the answer reverberate through the entire camp. *"And all the people answered together, and said, all that the Lord hath spoken we will do."* (Exodus 19:8). That was a bold exclamation, to do and keep something before they even knew what was contained in the covenant.

Israel erred greatly in saying, *"we will do."* They were given the option of living under grace and being brought along with God "on eagle's wings." They were to be that "peculiar treasure" unto God. This was going to be very difficult for the nation now that they had uttered such a presumptuous vow. Not just a few self-confident souls, but the entire company of twelve tribes as one, changed the course of Israel away from the holy covenant of grace.

> *"All that the Lord hath spoken we will do."* (Exodus 19:8).

It was a boldness that Christians today should beware of. To be vain about keeping all the law is something even profane to the Lord. It would be very hard to imagine every Christian professing all together unanimously such a vow. The Lord God tells Moses to come up to him alone in the Mount as he will come in a thick cloud as boundaries are set to keep the people separated from God. They were not allowed to touch the holy Mount lest they die. This is a great change, the exchange of God's mercies and grace for thunderings and lightenings on the Mount define this change and now surveillance of Israel's actions. The people, instead of being in loving arms are now trembling in fear of what they have done. Man in his sinful state cannot stand in the presence of a Holy God. Our God is a holy God and is intolerant of evil, especially that in mens' minds, words and deeds.

The lesson is therefore one of being mindful and able to pay back or fulfill a vow. In the case of the law, it is not in man to be able to fulfill such promise. Man is bankrupt in his soul and helpless as a sinner and making vows in regards to the law denies the true nature within man. Jacob was seen making a vow to God a tenth of his estate and made the promise at Bethel to honor and serve God.

Under the New Testament, a vow is either general to all Christians, as that which is made at Baptism; or particular and special, and when we bind ourselves to a great endeavor, to leave some sin, or perform some duty.[17]

CHAPTER 1: A HISTORY OF ISRAEL

A vow made to God is a serious and solemn thing and should not be made lightly. God warns:

> *"When thou vowest a vow unto God, defer not to pay it; for he hath no pleasure in fools: pay that which thou hast vowed."*
> (Ecclesiastes 5:4)

The lord tells us that it is better not to vow a vow if one does not intend to fulfill it. Evil vows should not be made. It was evil for the Jews to be bound to a vow to conspire to kill Paul in Acts 23:12.

There must be a competency to fulfill a vow before taking one on. The examples of Israel not keeping their vow are numerous in their infancy as a nation. Witness the golden calf, the broken tablets of stone, desecrating the Sabbath, broken ordinances, etc. The failures are overwhelming and how it must be when the fallen nature in man tries to vow a vow.

It is a joyful fact that our salvation does not rely on our pathetic vows and resolutions, but on the one time offering of our Lord and Saviour Jesus Christ. There is no need for any vows on our part, for they could not effect what the Lord has done through his members on the cross. The Israelites realized that their vow was a source of deep terror to them.

> *"If we hear the voice of the LORD our God any more, then we shall die."* (Deuteronomy 5:25)

They could not approach the Lord at the Mount. They had sinned and broken the law. They had tried to accomplish the impossible through pride. Their road would be very hard since the abandonment of the Lord's free and changeless grace for the works of the law.

The law itself is a revelation that even in an ideal world the Israelites would not be able to keep it. Human nature is deceitful. It fools one into believing that the natural man can please and obey God. The law was being given as a control on an uncontrollable old nature that will only go against God. No one can keep the law because the natural man cannot measure up to the standards of God. If someone says that they are able to keep the law that is an over-confidence that leads to arrogance and sin. Paul states;

> *"Because the carnal mind is enmity against God: for it is not subject to the law of God, neither indeed can be."* (Romans 8:7)

An unbeliever, not under the blood of Christ, is condemned by the law. He is in the flesh which does not please God, and is spiritually blind. One believes he is alive but because of the law the commandment comes and death in the spirit is the only reality. Only

CHAPTER 1: A HISTORY OF ISRAEL

conversion, will new light shine upon the law itself. The light of the converted makes one see that far from keeping the law, he is condemned by it. In the enlightened struggle with sin, Paul discovers:

> "I find then a law, that, when I would do good, evil is present with me." (Romans 7:21)

The law that Moses was given condemns mankind. Then Jesus came and met every demand of the law and imputes the righteousness of God. Jesus Christ is the righteousness of God. The believer is under complete righteousness that the law given on Mt. Sinai cannot find any fault in the believer. Paul recounts that there is no boasting or self in the law, but a law of faith which excludes any self or works, (Romans 3:27, 28). He also identifies the law of sin in his members, and which has victory over the mind, (Romans 7:21). Paul then warns us of the law of the mind which wants to do what is in the law of Moses but is unable due to the law of sin in the members, (Romans 7:23).

The power to overcome sin is with the law of the spirit. With the Holy Spirit of God the believer is delivered from the law of sin in our members, and is conscience clear from the condemnation of the Mosaic Law. It is the work of the Spirit in the yielded believer of the righteousness of the Saviour which Moses' Law demands.

> "For the law of the Spirit of life in Christ Jesus hath made me free from the law of sin and death." (Romans 8:2)

The Components of the Law

God made this covenant with Israel. Israel agreed to forego living by grace and live under the law. Again, this is a covenant made with the nation of Israel. The Church is not in view as Israel is told by God,

> "Remember ye the law of Moses my servant, which I commanded unto him in Horeb for all Israel," (Malachi 4:4)

The key component of the Mosaic Covenant was the Law of Moses, which contained a total of 613 commandments.[18]

There were blessings for obedience and curses for disobedience. Of the 613 commandments, 365 were negative commandments, things which were forbidden; 248 were positive commandments, things that should be done. [19]

Central to the covenant were the blood sacrifices instituted for the covering of sins. The blood was necessary, *"and almost all things are by the law purged with blood; and without shedding of blood is no remission."* (Hebrews 9:22)

CHAPTER 1: A HISTORY OF ISRAEL

> *"For the life of the flesh is in the blood: and I have given it to you upon the altar to make an atonement for your souls: for it is the blood that maketh an atonement for the sole."* (Leviticus 17:00)

The atonement made for sins in the Old Testament did not mean the removal of those sins. It was the blood of animals that covered the sins of the people as a result of animal sacrifice and the blood being applied. That would change when Jesus Christ, the Messiah would be the blood sacrifice for sins that removes sins. The O.T. blood sacrifice provided for forgiveness of sins and the restoration of fellowship with God.

The first seven chapters of Leviticus give the five different offerings for which an atonement was made for sins upon the altar.

1. The Burnt Offering (Leviticus 1). Abel, Noah, Abraham all made burnt offerings. The burnt offering is a picture of the person of Christ who is our substitute. It is Christ who has, "given himself for us as an offering and a sacrifice to God." (Ephesians 5:2)
2. The Meal Offering (Leviticus 2). This offering was usually offered together with one that involved the shedding of blood. The meal offering shows forth the humanity of Christ Jesus in his perfection. He was the perfect human.

We cannot keep the law. God sees us as imperfect and he demands perfection. Believers are consecrated in the perfection and perfect humanity of Christ.
3. The Peace Offering (Leviticus 3). The only way we can have peace with God in communion and fellowship is through the Lord Jesus Christ. We are brought into a closeness with the Father which is made possible by Christ. The peace officering, which is Christ Jesus, makes it possible for believers to have fellowship with the Father and with the Son.
4. The Sin Offering (Leviticus 4). The sin offering is related to the sin nature, something that every human being is born with. This offering addresses sin as an act and is what every person does because of his being a sinner by nature. Sin is a dreadful act with deadly consequences. Christ met the deep and desperate needs of the sinner in the sin offering. Christ is our sin offering on the cross. He became sin for us, all of our sins are put on him, and he saves us from our sins.
5. The Trespass Offering (Leviticus 5). This offering was for the crossing of the line with God. It had to do with swearing against the LORD and for touching the

unclean thing. The Christian comes in contact with the unclean world seeing and hearing things and not realize that he has become unclean. The Israelite sinner would bring a sacrifice to the priest for his atonement. The Christian prays for forgiveness and cleansing from God.

"If we confess our sins, he is faithful and just to forgive us our sins, and to cleanse us from all unrighteousness." (1 John 1:9)

Through the trespass offering there was forgiveness for the sinner who committed the trespass in ignorance.

The Law Fulfilled

"Think not that I am come to destroy the law, or the prophets: I am not come to destroy, but to fulfill." (Matthew 5:17)

The Lord Jesus Christ talked about the status of the law up until he was crucified. The law revealed the holiness and perfection of God. It was instituted for the Israelite to rule his life and to be distinct from the heathen. The law that kept the Gentiles from partaking in Jewish spiritual blessings, was to bring them to the redeeming grace of God through Mosaic Judaism. As a revelation of sin and the realization that man cannot attain the righteousness of the law on his own, the law was meant to drive on to faith.

To use the teaching of Matthew 5:17, 18 to make the case for the continuance of the Mosaic Law today is an enormous mistake. Doing so they must believe in the doing away with many of the commandments of the Law of Moses. This would necessarily include the commandments concerning the priesthood, all sacrifices, food and clothing laws. Many of the original 613 commandments no longer apply to anyone today. Any that consider themselves of the circumcism under law, and meaning that they are only under the moral commandments, then quoting Matthew 5: 17, 18 does not justify their case.

Many people go wrong today by trying to keep the ten commandments only; forgetting "these least commandments" (Matthew 5:19) include all 613.

> " *For it is written, cursed is every one that continueth not in all things which are written in the book of the law to do them.*"
> (Galatians 3:10)

Jesus was already fulfilling prophesies and the law while he was alive here on earth. In his living here he already had implied doing away with the law, rendering it inoperative. One place that this is found is Mark 7:19 and again in Matthew 15:17.

CHAPTER 1: A HISTORY OF ISRAEL

> *"Because it entereth not into his heart, but into the belly, and goeth out into the draught, purging all meats?"* (Mark 7:19)

It is pretty clear the Lord has done away with the dietary commandments. As prescribed by Moses many parts of the law are no longer applicable as rules to exert any authority over individuals and no longer the rule of life for believers.

The Lord reiterated the point:

> *"Do not ye yet understand, that whatsoever entereth in at the mouth goeth into the belly, and is cast out into the draught?"* (Matthew 15:17)

It can be seen that persisting in the claim that the Law of Moses, any part of it, is still in effect, while ignoring that the least of these commandments add up to 631, and still rejecting the idea that the law does not apply in the same manner as decreed by Moses, is theologically unsound.

All of this allows for the return to Matthew 5:17 where the Lord Jesus said he had not come to destroy the law, but to fulfill the law. Christ is the law's fulfillment.

Christ Fulfilled the Law

Christ Jesus came to give believers in Him the righteousness demanded by God for salvation that the law could not provide. God demanded perfect obedience to all of the law and Christ Jesus voluntarily fulfilled that obedience. His coming showed that the law stood firm as a rock, but the just are saved by the blood sacrifice of Christ by infinite mercy. The Father sees sinners and all His chosen as if all the law is fulfilled by them through the death of His Son. Christ has terminated the law over His people, for we are not under the law, but under grace.

> *"For Christ is the end of the law for righteousness to everyone that believeth."*
> (Romans 10:4)

The law is still in existence and is a perfect standard which every believer and unbeliever cannot attain to in our own strength. That makes a need for a Saviour necessary and mercy is obtained when Christ is received as Saviour.

Fulfill comes from the Greek word Pleroo, which means to fill, fill up, complete, to accomplish, perform fully, to fully satisfy. Christ not only fulfilled, or satisfied fully, all the types and prophecies by all His actions. Christ also performed complete obedience to the law of God by Himself and enforced and explained it fully by His doctrine. Therefore Christ has fully satisfied all the requirements completely of every part of the law.

CHAPTER 1: A HISTORY OF ISRAEL

Christians are not seeking life through the rules of the law as did the Old Testament Israelites . As such, today the saints are not under the law since Christ has taken us out of a condemning covenant and given saints the adoption into Him. The law cannot curse a believer, but blesses him through the righteousness that is Christ.

David described the blessedness of those whom God imputed righteousness without the works of the law, as Paul states:

"Saying, Blessed are they whose iniquities are forgiven, and whose sins are covered. Blessed is the man to whom the lord will not impute sin. (Romans 4:7,8)

The Tabernacle

The tabernacle was God's way of providing access by sinful man unto a holy God. After the giving of the law to Moses and before it was given to them, Moses took the blood of sacrificed oxen and sprinkled it on the Israelites. It was the blood of the covenant and it was shown to the people that there had to be a sacrifice. Moses returned back up to the mountain and God gives him the plan for the Tabernacle and the pattern for the garments of the high priest.

They needed precious metals; gold, silver, and brass, and for coverings blue, purple, scarlet cloth, linen, and goat's hair. Ram skins, badger skins, shittem wood, oil, sweet incense, onyx stones and other stones for the ephod and breastplate. God's purpose is to have a sanctuary, or holy dwelling place, in the presence of His people. The materials used in that sanctuary directly point to Christ, His Person, His work, and the precious fruit of that work. The pattern of the Tabernacle had to be followed exactly for it is a picture, a type, and a shadow of the Lord Jesus Christ.

> *"And the word was made flesh, and dwelt among us, (and we beheld his glory, the glory as of the only begotten of the Father,) full of grace and truth."* (John 1:14)

The Lord Jesus Christ dwelt amongst us here on earth. Dwelt means Tabernacle or a Tent, a covering. He covered His divinity in perfect flesh set apart for the work of the Father. The Tabernacle in the wilderness would be the dwelling place of the Shekinah glory of God. That would be a witness of his glory and His presence while Israel journeyed from Sinai to Canaan. The Tabernacle and its fixtures reveal symbolic, divine truth in all its details. The believer in Christ has in his heart a dwelling place for God, where he may dwell and sanctify. Saints are a type of the tabernacle as found in 1 Corinthians 6:19:

> *"What? Know ye not that your body is the Temple of the Holy Ghost, which is in*

CHAPTER 1: A HISTORY OF ISRAEL

you, which ye have of God, and ye are not your own?"

The Tabernacle in the wilderness pointed into the future when God would dwell with His people on earth.

"And he said unto me, Son of man, the place of my throne, and the place of the soles of my feet, where I will dwell in the midst of the children of Israel forever, and my holy name, shall the house of Israel no more defile," (Ezekiel 43:7)

Physical Description of the Tabernacle

God gave to Israel when they were in the desert, the Wilderness Tabernacle, which was the center of their lives and of which every part spoke of Christ.

The Tabernacle with its walls, curtains, and wood furniture covered in gold had a blood foundation. It was made up of 100 one hundred pound blocks of pure silver. The weight of the foundation was ten thousand pounds or five tons. These 100 blocks were arranged to form a rectangle, 45 feet long and 15 feet wide. The entire Tabernacle shows the Lord Jesus Christ and the believer in Christ. This foundation speaks of Jesus Christ and how everything is built upon Him. The silver foundation speaks of the blood of Jesus Christ which was shed for us and upon which rests our redemption. The payment of the silver used for the foundation was called a redemption tax which had to be paid by every adult Israelite under harsh penalties.

Silver in the Bible speaks of atonement, and atonement is always by blood. Atonement is "Kapar", in Hebrew which means to cover, and in the Old Testament the blood of animals sacrificed covered sin but did not take them away. This symbolically points to Jesus Christ whose shed blood as the Lamb of God, removes sins. The blood of animals was the payment for the covering of sins, whereas the blood of the lamb was payment which met the price for remission demanded by God. The atonement of Christ is unlimited and universal in its offer. [20]

The tabernacle in the wilderness was laid on this foundation of blood. The silver foundation is a beautiful picture of the blood of Christ shed on the cross of Calvary. Our Lord Jesus Christ purchased redemption for all who would believe. *"Ye are bought with a price."* (1 Corinthians 6:20) There is no salvation without the blood of Jesus. It is for the remission of sins by appropriation. This is the silver foundation; without the blood no one can be saved.

The Tabernacle had curtains at its entrance through which the priest entered. The four

CHAPTER 1: A HISTORY OF ISRAEL

walls were covered with curtains and had 100 sockets (96 were silver sockets for the wall boards, and four were under the pillars of the veil). Inside the gate which was on the east side was the Brazen altar, the largest piece of furniture in the Tabernacle. It was before the door of the Tabernacle itself and just inside the gate. The altar was made of wood covered with brass.

The Brazen Laver was the next piece within the outer court of the Tabernacle. It represents a place of sanctification, on being set aside for service to God. It was the only piece of furniture that had no measurements and this shows the infinite forgiveness of sin.

The main part of the Tabernacle was divided into two sections; the holy place, and the Holy of Holies. Besides the curtains it had pillars, hooks and bars. It had 48 boards which made up its walls. There were three coverings: one was made up of badger skins, porpoise or sea cow material. Another layer was of goat's hair with linen underneath. The last covering was a layer of ram's skins dyed red.

Inside the holy place was found the Table of Shewbread, the golden candlestick and lampstand, and the altar of incense which were before the veil separating the Holy Place from the Holy of Holies. The lampstand provided light in the windowless chamber, and was made from a single piece of gold. In each of its branches it had knobs, flowers, and on an almond shaped bowl for pure olive oil. The Table of Shewbread was made of wood covered in gold. It had rings at the corners for wooden staves covered in gold to carry twelve loaves of fine flour bread, representing the twelve tribes of Israel, were arranged on the table and replaced every week. The Altar of Incense had 4 horns at each corner.

The veil was the entrance to the Holy of Holies which contained the Ark of the Covenant and the Mercy Seat. The veil was made of woven cloth, of one piece, and held up by four pillars. It was a barrier between God and Man and only the High Priest would enter the Holy of Holies once a year. Beyond the veil was the Ark of the Covenant which was the center focus of the entire Tabernacle. Above and resting on top of the Ark was the Mercy Seat, made of gold hammered out to shape from one piece of pure gold. Two golden winged cherubs flanked each side of the Mercy Seat.

The Tabernacle was a type of the Church since it was the habitation of the glory of God. *"In whom ye also are builded together for an habitation of God through the Spirit."* (Ephesians 2:22). The tabernacle is a type and picture of the Christian since God refers to the believer as a temple of the Holy Ghost, or Tabernacle of God.

> *"Know ye not that ye are the Temple of God, and that the Spirit of God dwelleth in you?'* (1 Corinthians 3:16)

Christ in the Furniture of the Tabernacle

The Brazen Altar

The typology of Christ is found in every detail of the Tabernacle and points to His person and work. Christ has "tabernacled" among the Israelites and believers. *"And the Word was made flesh and dwelt among us."* (John 1:14). By being a merciful God, He provided a way for Israel to approach him in faith. When God was present in the camp the Israelites took comfort. Whenever they looked to the Tabernacle they knew that God would keep his promise to send a Redeemer.

The things that were types in the Old Testament were shadows of things that were to come. Coming through the east gate into the Court, a sinner would first encounter the altar of burnt offering. Our definition of the altar, being to lift up, points to the Cross of Calvary and to the Lord Jesus Christ. There He was lifted up to be a perfect sacrifice to God the Father. There was to be continual fire on the altar which showed that judgment of sin by God would always be ready to consume the animal payment for sin. Since Christ's sacrifice was needed only once the need for daily sacrifices is not necessary as it was for the Israelites. The Israelites had hope that as long as they had access to the brazen altar they could have forgiveness of their sins and be saved from God's judgment.

The altar itself was to be made of shittem wood, 7-1/2 feet long and 7-1/2 feet wide, foursquare, and 4-1/2 feet high, and it was covered in brass. This altar of brass was the place where sin was dealt with according to the divine judgment concerning it.[21]

The wood of the altar is a figure of Christ's humanity and in the brazen altar Christ is seen meeting the fire of divine justice. The brass was a symbol of righteousness that demands the judgment of sin.

The term "brass" is controversial for many in Christendom. The making of brass by melting copper with zinc was unknown in Old Testament times they (the experts) say. They say that smelting copper and tin to make bronze was prevalent from an early age. The inspired, translated word brass was used as early as in Genesis 4:22, through the instruments of the Tabernacle, the brasen Serpent of Moses, through the Bible all the way to Revelation 18:12,"...and all manner vessels of most precious wood, and of brass, and iron, and marble." The Israelites could have very well melted some copper ore containing small amounts of zinc and came up with some brass.

> "...these vessels, which Hiram made to King Solomon for the house of the LORD, were of bright brass." (1 Kings 7:45b)

The bright brass could well have been brass that was polished to a high degree. The simple fact is that the metal that is now referred to as bronze was the chief metal alloy of the ancient world. The word bronze, not being found in the Bible, is for a good reason. That being, the word bronze entered the English language in the 16th Century. The separation of bronze from brass did not become widespread until well into the 19th century.[22]

The fire in the Brasen Altar was ignited by God which fell directly from Heaven. God's love was seen by the Israelites at the altar. The atonement, or covering, for their sins looks forward to the Cross at Calvary. God had planned to allow His Son, Jesus Christ, to be sacrificed on the cross for the remission of sins of all who put him there.

The altar of burnt offering is the Cross. In the outer court of the Tabernacle it prevented sinners and sin from approaching the perfection and holiness that is God. The Israelite brought his sacrifice which shed its blood so that there was advancement. The Cross of Jesus Christ works as a way to God or it can be an obstruction for unrepentant sinners to God.

The Brazen Laver

The priests performed the rest of the steps which were steps to salvation and sanctification for service. This was performed by the priest by the means of the Laver which was used by the Water of Cleansing.

> *"And he made the laver of brass, and the foot of it of brass, of the looking-glasses of the women assembling."* (Exodus 38:8)

The use of brass typified firmness, solidity, incorruptibility, and power of endurance.[23]

This brass container, of unspecified dimensions, was filled with water for the priests to wash hands and feet in preparation for any service that pertained to the altar or the Tabernacle that was to be performed. The service to God required cleansing and it is the same for the Christian after salvation. God wants to use the believer for his service and he needs clean vessels for that. As Christians that are in the world but not of the world, worldly contact with the filth of the world is inevitable. We need to cleanse daily and for

CHAPTER 1: A HISTORY OF ISRAEL

that the Lord has made provision. Just as there were no specific instructions for the dimensions of the Laver, there is no limit to the cleaning provision of it. This is the same for the believer, for God will forgive us any sins we may commit after salvation plus the daily defilement we accrue. God has promised continual forgiveness and cleansing.

> *"If we confess our sins, he is faithful and just to forgive us our sins, and to cleanse us from all unrighteousness."* (1 John 1:9)

The Laver was made of brass and consisted of the upper basin and had a footstool or stand. The foot of the Laver shows the human nature which was perfect of Christ. It also relates to the earthly life of the believer whose head is Christ. The basin of the Laver was made of brass which spoke of the judgment of God. The brass of the Laver was of a particular kind as it was made of the mirrored looking glasses of the Israelite women.

> *"And he made the Laver of brass, and the foot of it of brass, of the looking glasses of the women."* (Exodus 38:8)

The women used highly polished brass for mirrors and they were asked to provide their mirrors for the Laver. These mirrors were brought from Egypt where they were used. It shows that looking at a mirror in a natural way never reveals our true condition. It shows flaws:

> "For the word of God is quick, and powerful, and sharper than any two-edged sword, piercing even to the dividing asunder of soul and spirit...and is a discerner of the thoughts and intents of the heart." (Hebrews 12:4)

The Table of Shewbread

So far the Brasen altar (Picture of the Cross, and the Brasen Laver (separation from the world), have been covered. The next step through the Tabernacle is the Table of Shewbread, the place of fellowship. After salvation, and being sanctified, the Christian enters fellowship with other believers, to feed on the Bread of Life (Christ), at the Table of Fellowship.

The table was made of shittem wood, which was an Asiatic Acacia tree with close-grained yellowish-brown wood.[24]

It was overlaid with pure gold and had a pure gold crown all around the top of it. These materials reveal that fellowship is possible through the human sacrifice (wood) and the divine perfection (gold) of Christ.

The table and the bread signify the Lord Jesus Christ. On the table were arranged two rows, six each of the showbread. The bread was flavored with frankincense. The twelve

CHAPTER 1: A HISTORY OF ISRAEL

loaves were for each of the twelve tribes of Israel and speaks of the living bread who came down from heaven, Christ.

> *"I am the living bread which came down from heaven; if any man eat of this bread, he shall live forever:"* (John 6:51)

It is the Lord Jesus who sustains us, and the Shewbread symbolizes His body. In this step saints are to seek fellowship with other saints for worship in the holy place. Believers are to gather around the Saviour and feed on Him and His word.

> *"And Jesus said unto them, I am the bread of life: he that cometh to me shall never hunger; and he that believeth on me shall never thirst."* (John 6:35)

The Golden Candlestick

The only light within the windowless holy place was provided by the Golden Candlestick.

> *"And thou shalt make a candlestick of pure gold: and six branches shall come out of the sides of it: and it shall be one beaten work of pure gold."* (Exodus 31a; 32a, 36b)

Since the material was gold, like all the articles in the holy place, the gold speaks of the Deity of Jesus Christ. The candlestick and the Mercy Seat were entirely made of gold. The candlestick typifies Jesus Christ, the Son of God, as the light of the world.

> *"I am the light of the world: he that followeth me shall not walk in darkness, but shall have the light of life."* (John 8:12)

It is the Lord Jesus Christ who came into the world and fulfilled prophesy after prophesy and revealed to Simeon who had waited for the one prepared before the face of all people;

> *"A light to lighten the Gentiles, and the glory of thy people Israel."* (Luke 2:32)

On top of the main shaft and the shafts of each of the six branches was an open almond blossom of gold. This is a picture of Christ as the source from where the Church comes from and is its eternal support. The Church firmly abides in Him as the Spirit flows through all its members, unified in the head. The almond blossoms remind of the rod of Aaron that budded. A dead branch was brought to life and bore fruit. Christ rose from the dead and the saints are His fruit.

Lamps containing olive oil were placed on the tops of the branches and the shaft. The oil was one of the things God had commanded the children of Israel to prepare and bring for the lamps of the candlestick. It was part of the offering for the construction of the Tabernacle.

> *"And thou shalt command the children of Israel, that they bring thee pure oil olive beaten for the light, to cause the lamp to burn always."* (Exodus 27:20)

The beaten oil represents the power of the Holy Spirit in the lives of the saints. Without it no light would proceed forth. God wants us to allow the Holy Spirit to shine forth God's light who is the Lord Jesus Christ.

The light shone upon the other articles in the Holy Place. God's light is the light in a dark place. It is the unlimited light of Revelation. The light of Christ's salvation reaches out to every person. It is unlimited in redemption, understanding, and in wisdom. Jesus Christ will cause the heavenly light to shine and burn with increased brilliancy. He, by the power of the Holy Spirit, causes the church to shine in bright and undimmed glory forever.

The Golden Altar of Incense

The Golden Altar of Incense is the third article of furniture that was located inside the Holy Place next to the Veil that led into the Holy of Holies. This was not an altar of sacrifice but a place of offering up the sweet smelling burnt incense in worship, praise, and prayer. The constant burning of the incense offering shows the work of Christ in heaven as our High Priest, as He continually intercedes in prayer on our behalf.

> *"And thou shalt make an altar to burn incense upon: of shittem wood shalt thou make it. And thou shalt overlay it with pure gold,"* (Exodus 30:13)

The wood in the altar again points to the perfect humanity of Christ, with the gold pointing to His Deity as the Son of God. It was the tallest piece in the Tabernacle depicting the highest form of worship possible, of prayer and intercession by a High Priest. The coals to be used for the burning of the incense were taken from the brazen altar, from fire that was divinely fired by God. It was holy fire that descended from heaven and which had consumed the sin sacrifice on the brazen altar. The fragrance ascending upwards appears before God which typified active priestly ministry in His presence. The altar and its fragrant cloud depict the high standing of our High Priest ministering in the glory of God. Jesus Christ, the Risen Saviour, a sweet odour in the dwelling place of God, mingles with the cloud of divine glory in the heavenly Tabernacle filled with holy fragrance.

> *"For such a high priest became us, who is holy, harmless, undefiled, separate from sinners, and made higher than the heavens;"* (Hebrews 7:26)

Jesus Christ is our advocate through which our prayers and supplications are presented to the Father. As symbolized in the golden altar Christ is our shining promise in help for our infirmities and without him there is no hope in offering incense. The incense gave the golden altar its purpose, and the perfection of Christ makes it possible for our prayers to be offered.

> *"And the Lord said unto Moses, take unto thee sweet spices, stacte, and onycha, and galbanum; these sweet spices with pure frankincense: of each shall there be a like weight:"* (Exodus 30:34)

The first three sweet spices were put together in equal weights, tempered together, pure and holy, and an equal weight of frankincense added together. This shows that Jesus is complete as the Godhead bodily, with no part of his character wanting in any aspect.

> The brazen altar speaks of the death of Christ; the golden altar speaks of the living, resurrected, ascended Lord Jesus Christ. The two altars, therefore, speak of the death and the resurrection, and constitute the full message of the Gospel.[25]

The incense altar was a place of prayer and intercession and a picture of Christ's constant intercession and prayers for the Church before the Father. Since the priests were defiled daily by contact with the earth beneath their feet, they needed constant washing in the Laver. They needed daily confession and intercession at the golden altar just as the saints do every day still being in a wicked world. We still have the old, sinful nature, as did the priests, and the incense rising at the golden altar was a reminder that they needed the intercession and the work at the golden altar. There can be no claim to sinless perfection or eradicating the old nature, for that is repudiated by the golden altar picturing the intercessory work of Christ Jesus today at the right hand of the Father.

The Veil

There were three entrances or doors into the Tabernacle. There was the gate in the Court (outer) which is a type of Christ by whom we enter into redemption.

> "And thou shalt make a veil of blue, and purple, and scarlet, and fine twined linen of cunning work: with cherubims shall it be made:" (Exodus 26:31)

There was a door or another hanging before the Holy Place. The veil that was before the Mercy Seat blocked entrance to all except the High Priest. This veil is a type of Christ by whom we enter into the very presence of God.

The inner veil hid the glory of God from man. It is a type of the human body of Christ.

> "Having therefore, brethren, boldness to enter into the holiest by the blood of Jesus,
>
> By a new and living way, which he hath consecrated for us, through the veil, that is to say, his flesh;" (Hebrews 10: 19, 20)

CHAPTER 1: A HISTORY OF ISRAEL

The veil was a thick curtain of fire linen colored blue, purple, and scarlet. The white linen illustrated the perfection of Christ's humanity. The dyed blue color spoke of Jesus Christ as God's Son. The purple cloth showed the kingly color of the King. The bright scarlet proclaimed that Christ is the Saviour. The cherubs that were embroidered into the veil branded it as the veil of the Lord Jesus Christ exclusively. The whole veil itself was heavy and strong and Josephus reported that horses tied to each side could not pull it apart.

The veil is symbolic of God's presence. Jesus in his human body revealed God and without His manifestation man would still be unable to see God. The only way the High Priest could enter into the most holy place was with the blood. He would enter the most holy place into the very presence of God. The veil blocked man's way and any irreverent entry to a holy God would result in death.

> *"The Holy Ghost this signifying, that the way into the holiest of all was not yet made manifest, while as the first tabernacle was yet standing."* (Hebrews 9:7)

This shield, or veil, between God and man remained so throughout the history of Israel. Christ, as represented by the veil came in the flesh just as human beings did. When Jesus

Christ died He made the way for entrance into the sanctuary for those who believe by faith.

> "Jesus when he had cried again with a loud voice, yielded up the ghost." (Matthew 27:50)

Jesus Christ layed down his life by dismissing His spirit. It was His will, dying by His own volition. When Christ died at Calvary, at that very moment the veil which was hanging in the Jerusalem Temple was torn, exposing the Holy of Holies making God's presence accessible to all who will come.

> "And behold, the veil of the temple was rent in twain from the top to the bottom;" (Matthew 27.51)

Christ's body was broken for us which opened the way for us to come to God. We have access directly to God through Jesus Christ. The veil was torn from top to bottom giving believers the privilege to encounter God's glory by his grace. The veil is symbolic of Jesus Christ and the renting of the Veil is symbolic of the death of Jesus Christ on the Cross.

The Ark of the Covenant

Inside the most holy place was found the Ark of the Covenant and its cover, the Mercy Seat. The Ark was the first holy article to be described and commanded by the Lord to be made. The Ark and the Mercy Seat were to be

CHAPTER 1: A HISTORY OF ISRAEL

God's throne of glory and power in the midst of Israel, and thus our great God wanted to establish Himself in the midst of his people. The Ark of the Covenant is the central and most important item in the entire Tabernacle. It is the most complete type and figure of the Lord and Saviour that the Israelites had. The Ark was a box made of Acacia wood three and three quarters feet long, two and a quarter feet wide, and two and a quarter feet high. It was covered all over in pure gold. Again, it speaks of Christ's nature, the wood for his perfect humanity, and the gold for his Deity.

The Ark speaks of who Christ Jesus is, and the other holy vessels in the Tabernacle show his works. We must know and recognize who Jesus is in his person in order to accept and receive him.

> *"But without faith it is impossible to please him: for he that cometh to God must believe that he is, and that he is a rewarder of them that diligently seek him."* (Hebrews 11:6)

Since the Lord Jesus Christ is perfect, He can be the perfect Saviour and this is reflected in the Ark. It was the pre-eminent part of the entire Tabernacle and necessary for the sacrifices, cleansing, fellowship, incense offerings, and forgiveness that went on there. It was because Christ is the essence of all the pieces of furniture in the Tabernacle. Without

Christ, and the Ark, as the center of worship, the whole idea of God in the midst of his people is dead. This is the reason for all of the dead churches, Christ is not the focal point of worship.

An Ark is a symbol for salvation and the Ark of the Covenant stood for salvation through the Lord Jesus Christ. Noah's Ark, Moses' Ark, and the Ark of the Covenant all typify the Lord Jesus Christ and his salvation. Noah's Ark provided shelter and safety as it transported life through the deadly flood waters. The little basket or Ark of Moses provided security for a baby and gave life to the one who would lead Israel out of Egypt and slavery. The Ark of Covenant provided a way of salvation and an atonement for the Israelites through the blood sacrifices, and now by the sacrifice of the Lamb of God. The Ark was with the Israelites through their history, through victories when in their possession and defeat when it was not in its rightful place. Our history as Christians is dependent on Christ's pre-eminence in our hearts and in our lives.

Contained inside the Ark were several items. The tables of the covenant or the Ten Commandments etched on stone, spoke of the Kingship of Christ who will return to earth again as the earth's King of Kings and Lord of Lords. The pot containing manna was also in

CHAPTER 1: A HISTORY OF ISRAEL

the Ark. Christ is the bread of life and the prophet of God. Aaron's rod was the third item in the Ark. This speaks of Christ being the High Priest speaking for man before God. Christ offered himself as a sacrifice and now he is at the right hand of God, resurrected from the dead, defending every saint in every moment.

The Ark was behind the veil, visited by the High Priest once a year. It was the place of supreme spiritual worship and fellowship which is open to every believer through Jesus Christ. It is where the saint can enter alone into the presence of a holy God and be alone with God. It is the spiritual inner sanctuary, behind the Veil, where the time spent alone with God is our spiritual strength and power in Him. It is the secret closet of prayer to be alone with God.

The Mercy Seat

> *"And thou shalt make a Mercy Seat of pure gold."* (Exodus 25:17a)

The Mercy Seat was a plank of pure gold 3 feet 9 inches long and 2 feet 3 inches wide. It was the lid or the top to the Ark of the Covenant.

> *"And thou shalt make two cherubims of gold, of beaten work shalt thou make them, in the two ends of the Mercy Seat."* (Exodus 25:18)

The Mercy Seat was a golden top for the Ark, with the two angels fixed to the ends, with their wings extended forward forming a throne for God. It formed a seat for the glory of God to dwell while communing with Moses for the Israelites.

> *"And there I will meet with thee, and I will commune with thee from above the Mercy Seat."* (Exodus 25:22a)

On the Day of Atonement, once a year, the High Priest would enter the Holy of Holies. He would wash at the Laver, take blood from the altar of burnt offerings, fire from the altar, along with incense from the golden altar and then proceed through the Veil into the presence of God.

Aaron, the High Priest, would sprinkle blood from his sacrifice on the altar and sprinkled the blood on the Mercy Seat for the atonement of his, his family's and all Israel's sins. This would be over the law which called for judgment and death and when the glory of God came down over the Ark, God would not judge the broken law but instead saw the atoning blood and was appeased. Without the blood upon the Mercy Seat, the Ark was an item of severe judgment upon Israel, but though the blood and mercy of God it had become a throne of grace.

CHAPTER 1: A HISTORY OF ISRAEL

Year after year the blood had to be applied which was only a covering for sins, it could never take them away. This was only a type of the work of the Savior which was to come. The total price for sin must be fulfilled by God's Lamb, the Son of God Jesus Christ. Only His precious blood could pay the price of sin, what was done in the Tabernacle was only a shadow of the Cross of Christ.

> *"But in those sacrifices there is a remembrance again made of sins every year.*
>
> *By the which will we are sanctified through the offering of the body of Jesus Christ once for all."* (Hebrews 10: 3.10)

This will end the journey through the Patriarchal History of Israel from before it was a country or a people of God to becoming a nation vested with rules and laws and God as its head. It is the introduction of divine revelation and salvation to the world through the nation of Israel. The Israelites were the chosen people of God to be an example and a light to all the heathens. The Jews were to hear God's words and write them down in what is known to us as the Bible. Perhaps, most important of all, the Jews were chosen to bring forth the Messiah, the Lord Jesus Christ, the Saviour of all mankind.

The Jewish Nation fulfilled the promise of God that he made through Abraham to be a blessing to all nations which blessed Israel. They were to be that light of God and though they failed at many things they intermittently showed the power of God on Earth. They were entrusted with God's words and did faithfully execute the inscripturation of those words. The Messiah, Jesus Christ, was born of a Jewish virgin, lived, ministered, died for the sins of the world, was buried, rose from the dead, and ascended back into heaven to be with the Father. Christ will return again and the unconditional, everlasting covenant concerning the land and people of Israel will be fulfilled.

The roles of the Church, the Nation of Israel, Israel's future, and Israel now will be explored in Paul's writings to the Romans in Romans 9, 10, 11.

CHAPTER 2
Romans 9

Introduction

The Israelites had entered the Promised Land just as God had promised. Around 1234 B.C. they began their conquest for the land in Canaan. By 926 B.C. the nation is divided into the Kingdom of Israel consisting of 10 tribes in the north, and the Kingdom of Judah in the south. In 722 B.C. the tribes of Israel begin to be deported to Assyria. The Kingdom of Israel ceases to exist. By 597 B.C. the Kingdom of Judea is carried off to Babylon to begin the 70 year captivity. After the seventy year bondage ended a representation of the whole nation re-gathered again to rebuild Jerusalem and the Temple. For Babylon:

> "I will punish the king of Babylon, and that nation, saith the Lord, for their iniquity, and the land of the Chaldeans, and will make it perpetual desolations." (Jeremiah 25:12)

Then in 70 A.D. the Jews were scattered to all nations of the earth. The Romans under the Emperor Vespasian's son Titus destroyed Jerusalem and burned the Temple. The Jewish people, as well as Jewish and Gentile converts were cast out of Israel. Known as the

Diaspora, the Jews who were cast out and scattered into the whole world lasted for 1900 years until Israel was reborn as a nation in 1948.

> *"And when ye shall see Jerusalem compassed with armies, then know that the desolation thereof is nigh.* (Luke 21:20)

This destruction of Jerusalem and the Temple happened in 70 A.D.

> *"And Jerusalem shall be trodden down of the Gentiles, until the times of the Gentiles be fulfilled."* (Luke 21:24)

Most of Jerusalem is back in Jewish hands, but parts of it are not. This will not be fulfilled until Jesus returns.

It should be noted that 70 A.D. is the traditional for the start of the Diaspora, or scattering of the Jews. Actually this dispersion had been going on since the time of Pompey (106-48 B.C.), who had captured many Jews and carried most of them off to the slave markets of Italy.[1]

The Jews headed for safer ports and before long every Roman city, even as far as Britain, had a Jewish community. Rome was very stern, but tolerance of the Jews prevailed. They did attempt the de-politization of Judaism, which led to revolts by the Jews. Roman Emperor Trajan (A.D. 98-117) put down many of the smaller unknown revolts, one of which was noteworthy was the destruction of the Jewish community at Alexandria, Egypt.

Hadrian, the next Roman Emperor to confront the Jews, prevented them from rebuilding the Temple and prohibited circumcision. A Jew named Simon, who took the name Bar Kokhba, drove the Romans back and held them at bay for two years (132-134 A.D.). However, the Romans prevailed and the destruction was much worse than the Titus was of 70 A.D. Hadrian wiped out many Jewish communities and the Bar-Kokhba Revolt ended and the dispersion became a torrent.

A Theodicy

The "Theological 'isms'" book by Smith tells us that theodicy is: the doctrine of the origin of evil. A proper view of theodicy recognizes that evil is privative. That is, evil is the absence of God's goodness, just as darkness is the result of the absence of light.

> "Therefore, by definition, evil has always existed potentially as the privation of God's righteousness. This is not dualism because evil is only potential, not actual."[2]

It is somewhat more simply stated in "The Compact Dictionary of Doctrinal Words" by Miethe as:

Attempts to explain why evil exists in the world when God is all-loving, all-powerful and justice itself. Many who do not believe in God cite the problem of evil as an argument against God's existence, but the issue is crucial to Christian hope as well as to evangelism.

A theodicy is a defense of God and a vindication when it is realized that He is a just God. Paul sought to vindicate God in the theodicy of Romans 9-11. That means that Paul sought to clear God's name from blame and oppose the opposition by proclaiming the God of the Bible as true. Paul approached the problem from God's view. Theodicy is from two Greek words, "theo," God and "dike", meaning judgment or right. God is right in his judgment and justice because He is righteous and just.

Therefore, this is a study of evil in the world, when things are bad and bad things happen, can these be blamed on God? These very questions are raised in the light of the sovereignty of God. How can a holy and loving God, in control of all things, allow evil to exist? The questions are asked as described ad nauseam. The Bible does not seek to justify God's actions. God has willed the existence of evil and the good, all to his glory.

> *"I form the light, and create darkness: I make peace, and create evil. I the Lord do all these things."* (Isaiah 45:7)

CHAPTER 2: ROMANS 9

Evil is the Hebrew, "Ra", and translates, as sorrow, wretchedness, adversity, afflictions, calamities, but "Ra" is never translated as sin. What is meant here for evil is that He created the sorrows, etc. to be sure fruits of sin. There are other theodicies in the Bible but Paul presents a classic argument for an explanation of why God allows suffering and sorrow.

So what is the theodicy in regards to the Jewish people? The Jews are God's chosen people and Paul's defense of God regards Israel in the past, Israel in the present, and God's future Israel. Paul had to confront the Jews' disbelief and non-recognition of Jesus Christ as their promised Messiah. God has set aside the nation of Israel for his purposes temporarily, but he has not rejected this chosen people outright. If God has indeed rejected Israel, then Christians and Jews alike must fear that God cannot be anything other than a fraud.

If God's promises prove empty to Israel then God is a faithless God. If God could be faithless to Israel, then Christians everywhere need to wonder whether God will be faithful to us. God has not gone back on His promises, they are still on track to be fulfilled. God has always preserved a believing remnant in Israel, and the Apostle Paul is a representative of the redeemed remnant. It is true to say that God has reserved a chosen remnant of the

Jewish people today. Christians should rightly relate to Israelites today and evangelize as many as God wants to be redeemed by grace. The rest will enter the Tribulation to fulfill Daniel 9:24, the seventy weeks of Daniel.

God will preserve those who are a remnant of Israelites now and the remnant he will save out of the Tribulation. What he did in preserving Elijah serves as an example. Known as the Elijah Complex today it warns against a depression amidst threatening circumstances. Elijah had run away when he learned from Ahab that Jezebel had put a hit out on him. In the wilderness, overcome by depression Elijah cried out: *"It is enough; now, O Lord, take away my life;"* (1 Kings 19:4).

Elijah was so upset he took off and stayed on Mt. Horeb for fourty days and fourty nights. The Lord asked Elijah, *"what doest thou here, Elijah?"* (1 Kings 19:9). Elijah thought that he was all alone, the only one who was uncompromised. He had a spiritual claustrophobia. He had lost all hope, but God reassured him that the war would be won and that he had 7000 that were faithful and had not worshipped Baal. God is to be depended on for our salvation and to overcome any Elijah complex with depression or feelings of aloneness that may develop.

Paul and Romans 9

Romans Chapters one through eight contain doctrinal teachings. Chapter nine through eleven are dispensational. Chapter nine concerns God's dealing with Israel in its past. Chapter ten is focused on Israel in the present, chapter eleven points to the future of Israel.

Paul had considered two questions in Romans 1-8. First, how does one become justified with God, and second, how do the redeemed walk in this life after God has clothed you in His righteousness?

Paul wanted Chapters 9, 10, and 11 to bring the Jews of his time into an understanding of Christianity, who Jesus was, and what He had done for them historically in the past, present, and what their future held. All it did was have the effect that Paul and Christianity were robbing them of their expected inheritance of the Kingdom of God. God had hardened their hearts because they would not believe and trust Jesus Christ as God.

God brought about the nation of Israel to be an everlasting nation thoroughly participating in His plan for them through the covenants and promises. Israel stands alone in these distinctions as Jews where all other nations and peoples are known as Gentiles.

Romans 9

Paul Deeply Sorrowful. Vs. 1-3

1. *I say the truth in Christ, I lie not, my conscience also bearing me witness in the Holy Ghost.*
2. *That I have great heaviness and continued sorrow in my heart.*
3. *For I could wish that myself were accursed from Christ for my brethren, my kinsmen according to the flesh:*

Paul starts this section of Scripture by affirming the truth. He is not a liar. If someone is lying he is not going to be credible. Paul had a difficult message for the Jews and they had to believe him.

> *"Now the things which I write unto you, behold, before God, I lie not."* (Galatians 1:23)

Paul did not take lightly speaking before God. Here he is taking the gospel to a mixed congregation, but he is especially aware of his position with the Jews. He had been schooled by the great Gameliel, the top theologian of the Pharisees. Paul founded the church at Rome but was in contact with it by long distance. The Church at Rome may have first been begun by "strangers of Rome, Jews, and proselytes," (Acts 2:10b) who had returned to Rome from Jerusalem on Pentecost. Its main body was made up therefore of Jews recruited and converted form Judaism. Paul had to be careful since most Jews knew him as the Chief Pharisee. *"That after the most straitest sect of our religion I lived a Pharisee."* (Acts 26:5b). It was on the road to Damascus that Paul answered the call of Jesus Christ and became a Christian and went forward to preach the Gospel. "For thou shalt be his witness unto all men of what thou hast seen and heard." (Acts 22:15).

Paul knew he was saved and in Christ, hence his strength in Christ and confidence. This double statement that this is truth, not a lie, confirms and establishes God's truth.

> *"Whereunto I am ordained a preacher, and an apostle, (I speak the truth in Christ and lie not;) a teacher of the Gentiles in faith and verity."* (1 Timothy 2:7)

Paul states that his conscience, that inner part of us that is a discerner of God's will and our own thoughts and actions, is in the power of the Holy Ghost. It had to be clear to the Jews that what he was going to say was from God about the fact that they were rejecting the Lord Jesus Christ the Saviour of the world.

Paul had been in the unbelieving Jews' place, persecuting the Church, haling Christians everywhere. He felt the same once as they did now and it truly hurt him to see his countrymen rejecting so great a salvation. He had great heaviness and continual sorrow in his heart for them. This is how Jesus feels as he sees continual ignorance toward His sacrifice on the cross for sinners. As Christians we need to have the same deep affection for the lost sinner and desire to tell them about Jesus Christ.

Paul then makes his bold statement that he wishes to be accursed from Christ, from his own salvation, in order for his brethren, his kinsmen according to the flesh, the Jews to be saved. The Greek word for accursed is "Anathema" which means:

> "A thing set up or laid by in order to be kept; specifically, an offering resulting from a vow, which after being consecrated to a god was hung upon the walls or columns of the temple, or put in some other conspicuous place; a thing devoted to God without hope of being redeemed, and if an animal to be slain; therefore a person or thing doomed to destruction; a curse; a man accursed, devoted to the direst of woes."[3]

To put this in perspective Paul had a Christian desire for lost souls to be saved. His word wish, in Verse 3, is the Greek "euchomai", and it means a prayer or vow, and Paul prayed,

> "if we ask anything according to his will, he heareth us:" (1 John 5:14b)

Paul was praying that he could bring the fact that Jesus Christ was selfless in his sacrifice for all. Paul knew his own wish was not sufficient, but in the Jews' works based religion that contrast was God's own declaration for salvation.

Physical Israelites Vs. 4,5

1. *Who are Israelites; to whom pertaineth the adoption, and the glory, and the covenants, and the giving of the law, and the service of God, and the promises;*

2. *Whose are the fathers, and of whom as concerning the flesh Christ came, who is overall, God blessed forever. Amen.*

Paul relates that the past benefits God bestowed on the Israelites were who they were, had they forgotten? If, as they said, they were followers of Moses they needed to remember the adoption by God of them as a chosen and blessed people. They had to realize that just because God chose them and gave them these other advantages did not guarantee salvation. The adoption went from Abraham, Isaac, and Jacob and down the line to the Lord Jesus Christ. Somehow the Jews got sidetracked and missed Jesus Christ. Paul keeps asking, who are Israelites? They had a close association with God. They had the Shekinah Glory which rested on the Mercy Seat in the Wilderness Temple and into the first Temple. This presence is now withheld.

They had and still have the Covenants that bound them as a people to God. The law was given to them on Sinai, which they broke and which necessitates a new covenant. The Jews had the divine appointment for service in the Tabernacle and in the Temples. Now the hope is for a new Temple and renewed service, the promises of the land, a king, and the Saviour Jesus Christ.

The Israelites were the physical descendants of Abraham, Isaac, and Jacob, but that did not guarantee salvation. Most of all Christ came of a virgin who was a Jew, of their own blood which was His humanity made Him a Jew. However, we know Him no longer after the flesh but He is over all, God who is blessed forever. Paul calls Jesus Christ the Messiah, God, but they didn't get it. This deeply grieved Paul as it does Christ, and should truly concern Christians.

Israel Identified. Vs. 6-13

1. Not as though the word of God hath taken none effect. For they are not all Israel, which are of Israel:

2. Neither, because they are the seed of Abraham, are they all children: but, in Isaac shall thy seen be called.

3. That is, they which are the children of the flesh, these are not the children of God: but the children of the promise are counted for the seed.

CHAPTER 2: ROMANS 9

> 4. For this is the word of promise, at this time will I come, and Sarah shall have a son.
> 5. And not only this; but when Rebecca also had conceived by one, even by our father Isaac;
> 6. (For the children being not yet born, neither having done any good or evil, that the purpose of God according to election might stand, not of works, but of him that calleth;)
> 7. It was said unto her, the elder shall serve the younger.
> 8. As it is written, Jacob have I loved, but Esau have I hated.

Paul is defending God and his word here. He looked around the saw unbelief, but he also saw God's powerful word changing lines, building the Church, and leading him on.

The ones that are not Israel are the Jews who sided with the Pharisees against Paul and against Christ as the Messiah. There was a remnant then that believed and these were incorporated into the Church. There are no Gentiles being mentioned here by Paul, these are remnant believer Jews and unbelieving, natural descendant from Abraham Jews.

In Verse 7 the seed of Abraham includes non-Jews born of Abraham and Isaac, the son of promise. So to be the natural offspring of Abraham was no guarantee that a person was a child of promise. Abraham's two sons are battling still today. Isaac, the child of promise represents Israel, and Ismael, the child of the flesh, represents the Arabs. God chose Isaac to be the line that God's seed shall be called. Christ did not come through Ismael's seed.

The children of the flesh in Verse 8, are simple the Ismaelites, and they are not the children of God, reject the Lord Jesus Christ, call Mohammed their prophet, and propagate a false religion. The children through Isaac are the children of the promise and are counted for seed. But the children of the flesh, born of Ismael, whose mother was a concubine and handmaiden of Sarah, are not the children of God, or saved by faith. No one is automatically saved by being a Jew, and that is not being taught here.

The word of promise of the seed God made to Abraham, which is the Lord Jesus Christ, will be the child born of Sarah. The Lord made good on his promise that Sarah would conceive, even though she was well past childbearing years. Nothing is too hard for the Lord. (Genesis 18:14). Verse 10 continues the line of the Saviour through Rebecca, the wife of Isaac, and she had Jacob and Esau. It is important to state that God chose Jacob over Esau to be the seed line. This was according to his purpose by election, or sovereign choice. It was the Lord's choosing which was not according to works. This was not election unto

CHAPTER 2: ROMANS 9

salvation as the Calvinists twist the idea of God's freedom to choose. The hyper-Calvinist error on election says you cannot be saved if you are not part of the elect. To them Christ died only for the elect, redefining the words in John 3:16; world of elect, whosoever the elect, and perish of the elect. If you are not of the elect, God did not choose you for salvation according to His sovereign election, therefore God does not love the non-elect and did not die for their sins.

Verse 12 speaks of the law of the firstborn. The first child born would own the birthright, gain the main blessing and the greatest inheritance. Deuteronomy 21:17 explains the double portion to the firstborn male. God needed to change this order on occasion. The prime example is the Lord Jesus Christ, who is referred to as the last Adam (1 Corinthians 15:49), replacing the first Adam. God chose Isaac, the younger over the older Ismael, and Jacob was favored over Esau. As for Joseph's sons, Ephraim, the younger, was chosen or Manasseh. God's sovereignty is supreme in His choosing for His purposes.

Verse 13 refers to Malachi 1:2,3. Esau was Jacob's brother but Jacob had to be chosen to be the line of Christ Jesus because it was according to His plan and it was His choice. For Christians it is true that the Lord Jesus Christ is first in our hearts above family, friends, and thing. If He is not we are mired in idolatry.

God's Choice. Vs. 1-18

1. What shall we say then? Is there unrighteousness with God? God forbid.
2. For he saith to Moses, I will have mercy on whom I will have mercy, and I will have compassion on whom I will have compassion.
3. So then it is not of him that willeth, nor of him that runneth, but of God that showeth mercy.
4. For the scripture saith unto Pharaoh, even for this same purpose have I raised thee up, that I might shew my power in thee, and that my name might be declared through all the earth.
5. Therefore hath he mercy on whom he will have mercy, and whom he will he hardeneth.

Verse 14 engages the defense of God which is the heart of the theodicy of Romans. Why would there be anything that we should say, Paul asks. The unbeliever or the atheist would be saying, there goes God again. God already has told Moses that He has the right to show mercy on whom He chooses, for it is God's choice not mans. God has chosen Jacob before he had done any good, and rejected, or hated Esau for no bad in him, so of course man

CHAPTER 2: ROMANS 9

would think that an injustice had been done on the part of God. But God said to Moses:

> "And will be gracious to whom I will be gracious, and will show mercy on whom I will show mercy. (Exodus 33:19b)

Mercy is a negative term. Mercy is not getting something that we deserve. Because of God's mercy we do not get hell and damnation if we have faith in the Lord Jesus Christ. This is a serious accusation against God, saying that there is unrighteousness with Him. Why does the apostate world blame God and always point a finger at Him and condemn Him? Even the Jews in Paul's time were hurling these accusations. For the believer to have bad things happen, it would work for the good and bring one closer to God. The unsaved need more powerful things to happen to bring understanding and to a place of repentance. *"Shall not the judge of all the earth do right?"* (Genesis 18:25b).

As God deals with Israel in the past it is remembered that through the law God rewarded obedience with blessing and a curse for disobedience. Since this was God's just way, it would be unjust for him to judge on any other basis. So, God does not judge on an unjust basis, it is righteous for He is righteous.

In Verse 16, God reiterates that it is not man's job to show mercy. Justification is God's domain, not sinners. Man's will, says God, is incapable and weak. God must have His will to show mercy on whom He will show mercy. It is not in man.

> "O Lord, I know that the way of man is not himself: it is not in man that walketh to direct his steps." (Jeremiah 10:23)

What was done by God's will was through mercy on the human race, to redeem it according to His plan. We did not deserve it, no one does, it is God's sovereign choice to give mercy to all.

In Verse 17 God shows His exercise of His sovereignty by raising up Pharaoh for His special purpose. The purpose was to show the power of God in Egypt by hardening the heart of Pharaoh and allowing the destruction of their gods and their might. God wanted to be known in Egypt by His name and His righteous judgement, God brought about all the events in Egypt, and His willing choices, and Paul illustrates for us this loving doctrine. This display of power and might got out and allowed God to graciously bestow mercy on Gentiles who wished to believe Him and escape His wrath.

CHAPTER 2: ROMANS 9

Quit finding Fault. Vs. 19-24

1. Thou wilt say then unto me, who doth he yet find fault? For who hath resisted his will?

2. Nay but, O man, who art thou that repliest against God? Shall the thing formed say to him that formed it, why hast thou made me thus?

3. Hath not the potter power over the clay, of the same lump to make one vessel unto honour, and another unto dishonor?

4. What is God, willing to shew his wrath, and to make his power known, endured with much longsuffering the vessels of wrath fitted to destruction:

5. And that he might make known the riches of his glory on the vessels of mercy, which he had afore prepared unto glory,

6. Even us, whom he hath called, not of the Jews only, but also of the Gentiles?

Here there six questions in a row, still concerning God's sovereign will in dealing with the Jews past and in Paul's time and also including Gentiles which have been brought into God's salvation.

In Verse 19 the unsaved are addressed as continuing to find fault with God which never ends. There is no understanding. The devil delights in influencing people to confront God. Over and over man spews out hatred for God while never taking responsibility for his hardening of his heart. Accusers stand with Satan in resisting God and blame God for making them what they are. What right does man have in opposing God, the One who made and formed them. It should have been clear, especially from the example of Pharaoh, how beneficial it would be to remain obedient to and not question God.

In Verse 21 God says He is the potter and Israel was the clay. Man is the created being, God is the creator. God has power over the clay, which is Israel.

> "But now, O Lord, thou art our father; we are the clay, and thou our potter; and we are the work of thy hand." (Isaiah 64:8)

Man is in constant rebellion against God. It is not fair to accuse God of creating man and as a result blame God for all our sin. God takes man, the clay, and in His case Israel, and forms it to take forward His light and His purpose into a dark world. It is God's right to how the vessel is formed. God determines the destination of the formed clay, either to honor Him or for some lesser purpose. This is how Moses, representing the children of Israel and Pharaoh of Egypt is formed by the potter. It is God's mercy that makes one vessel unto honor for His honorable use. It is also the potter's right to make a vessel for dishonorable common use.

CHAPTER 2: ROMANS 9

In Verse 22 Paul makes the case for God concerning what he calls the vessels of wrath. God shows his wrath to those that deserve it, but He is longsuffering, that is He puts up with man's obstinance for a long time before taking righteous action. Wrath is a tool God uses to make His power known to those Paul calls vessels of wrath that were fitted to destruction. The Egyptians were especially fitted to carry out the purpose of showing God's power.

The reason for showing His power and might is revealed in Verse 22. That God will make known to His people the riches of His glory. The Israelites were recipients of this mercy and grace and glory. This is the contrast, one of glory and one of destruction. Rejecting God leads to the destruction of hell. One can have spiritual riches with God by believing in Him, serving Him, and earning crowns with love of the Lord. In the Lord Jesus Christ we have riches untold and this is what Moses understood.

> *"Esteeming the reproach of Christ greater riches than the treasures in Egypt: for he had respect unto the recompence of the reward."* (Hebrews 11:26).

In Verse 24 Paul addresses the call of the Lord Jesus Christ on our lives. When the Lord Jesus Christ came and was born of a virgin, He came to preach to the house of Israel. But He has called the Gentiles in the whole world to salvation for it is a universal call. He has saved the vessels of mercy, out of the Jews and the Gentiles. The Jews had a remnant is Paul's time as there is now, and they and the saved Gentiles make up the Church.

Rejection of Israel Vs. 25-29

1. *As he saith also in Osee, I will call them my people, which were not my people; and her beloved, which was not beloved.*

2. *And it shall come to pass, that in the place where it was said unto them, ye are not my people; there shall they be called the children of the living God.*

3. *Esaias also crieth concerning Israel, though the number of the children of Israel be as the sand of the sea, a remnant shall be saved.*

4. *For he will finish the work, and cut it short in righteousness: because a short work will the Lord make upon the earth.*

5. *And Esais said before, except the Lord of Sabaoth had left us a seed, we had been as Sodoma, and been made like unto Gomorrha.*

Verse 25 continues the stating of God's gracious call of salvation to the Gentiles since his beloved people rejected the Lord Jesus Christ. The call is extended to all, Jew and Gentile that will believe. Osee refers to Hosea

CHAPTER 2: ROMANS 9

and the scripture where God mentioned the Gentiles being his people.

> *"And I will say to them which were not my people, thou art my people, and they shall say, thou art my God."* (Hosea 2:23b)

God is opening up the opportunity to the world to be His beloved children. This is God's grace for those who were lost and had no hope, but now can be genuinely saved and trust in the Lord Jesus Christ. Both Jew and Gentile can be made:

> *"To the praise and glory of his grace, wherein he hath made us accepted in the beloved."* (Ephesians 1:6).

"And it shall come to pass," God says in Verse 26 and what God says is going to happen, we can take him at His word that it will come to pass. God's people, a mixture of saved Jews, and called Gentiles, whoever are genuinely saved, are the children of the Living God. Israel at the time of Hosea's prophecy was Jehovah's adulterous wife, turned away from God. It was to come in the future that:

> *"The children of Judah, and the children of Israel be gathered together, and appoint themselves one head, and they shall come up out of the land:"* (Hosea 1:11).

Now a new people will be called, the Gentiles.

> *"But ye are a chosen generation, a royal priesthood, a holy nation, a peculiar people: that ye should shew forth the praises of him who hath called you out of darkness into his marvelous light:" (1 Peter 2:9)*

Isaiah proclaimed in anguish about the physical and spiritual state Israel found itself in. Only a remnant of saved Jews exists today. Only a remnant will be saved in the Tribulation period. Paul was of the remnant then and Christians who were formally Jews are the remnant today.

> *"And the remnant that is escaped of the house of Judah shall get again take root downward, and bear fruit upward. (2 Kings 19:30)*

The promise of mercy is for a preserved remnant of Jews who have faith. It has always been so. His mercy extended to only a chosen few as Verse 27 quotes Isaiah 10:22-23 as being the case. This is true for the Tribulation, which is what Paul relates to in V48. The Lord's short work will be the Tribulation:

> *"To finish the transgression, and make an end of sins, and to make reconciliation for iniquity, and to bring in everlasting righteousness, and to seal up the vision and prophecy, and to anoint the most holy."* (Daniel 9:24)

Verse 29 affirms the history of remnant preservation. Paul quotes Isaiah 1:9:

> *"Except the Lord of hosts had left unto up a very small remnant, we should have been as Sodom, and we should have been like unto Gomorrah."*

It should be noted that the Lord promised to save those two cities if he could find a godly remnant of ten. That kind of remnant did not exist so Sodom and Gomorrah were completely destroyed. So, Israel having possessed godly remnants down through the ages has been their saving grace for God's mercy.

Reality and Reason. Vs. 30-33.

1. What shall we say then? That the Gentiles, which followed not after righteousness have attained to righteousness, even the righteousness which is of faith.

2. But Israel, which followed after the law of righteousness, hath not attained to the law of righteousness.

3. Wherefore? Because they sought it not by faith, but as it were by the works of the law. For they stumbled at that stumbling stone.

4. As it is written, behold, I lay in Sion a stumbling stone and rock of offence: and whosoever believeth on him shall not be ashamed.

Verse 30 highlights the unbelief of Israel and why that has put them behind up until today. The Gentiles followed after their own lusts, turning their cities into lust pots full of immorality. They were on their own destructive paths with righteousness and the love of God never entering their minds. But when Paul and the other apostle preached the Word, many of the Gentiles dropped their pagan ways and followed Christ. These Gentiles were a law unto themselves until they heard of Jesus Christ. The only way they would have received righteousness was a genuine faith in the finished work of Jesus Christ on the cross. They have attained the faith. The word attained is from the Greek," Katalambano", which means to take, seize, to lay hold of. The pagans turned from their sinful ways and grabbed onto salvation and were locked in willingly by the Holy Spirit.

In Verse 31 the Israelites did not attain faith through the law of righteousness. That word for attained in the Greek is "phthano" which means to come suddenly and unexpectedly. This is what the Jews did not do, though a small remnant did. The Jews did pursue the law of righteousness with a lot of zeal and vigor but never reached the goal of simple faith. This seemed unjust and futile to them after putting out such a great effort.

Verse 32 has the answer to this quandary from Paul. He asks how come there is so much confusion on all their faces, but the reality is you cannot attain Christ by your own effort. They could not trust God and accept the only

CHAPTER 2: ROMANS 9

way to righteousness was through his Son, the Lord Jesus Christ. The Jews trusted in their feigned obedience to the Law of Moses, which cannot save anybody. No one can keep the law to become righteous except for Christ Jesus who was the end to the law.

> "For the law was given by Moses, but grace and truth came by Jesus Christ." (John 1:17)

The last verse starts with the words "it is written" and they point to Bible preservation of the Hebrew, Aramaic and by extension the Greed words God gave to us.

> "The Greek word is GEGRAPTAI. It is the perfect tense of the verb GRAPHO. The perfect tense in Greek deals with three points of time: 1- the past, 2-the present, and 3-the future. In this case, the Old Testament words alluded to in Isaiah 28: 16 were written in the past, preserved right down to the time Paul quoted them, and will be preserved on into the future."[4]

With the heart we believe unto righteousness and confess by the grace of the Lord Jesus Christ with our mouths. The Lord lay in Sion a stumbling block and a rock of offense to believe. The Jewish people and leaders in Christ's time taught that it was by the woks of the law that we are justified. Sion is a hill in Jerusalem, the city of David. The Jews did not believe in Jesus and He was to them a stumbling stone and a rock of offence.

> "And he shall be for a sanctuary: but for a stone of stumbling and for a rock of offence to both the houses of Israel," (Isaiah 8:14)

> "And whosoever shall fall on this stone shall be broken: but on whomsoever it shall fall, it will grind him to powder." (Matthew 21:44)

Those who fall on the stone, which is Jesus Christ, shall be saved and will not be ashamed. These Jews who rejected the preaching of salvation by faith through grace will stumble at the foot of the stone. This broke Paul's heart and he grieved at the failure of his kinsmen.

CHAPTER 3
Romans 10

Introduction

Paul in Romans 10 moves on to discuss the present time lost condition of the Jews. As it was brought out in Romans 9, the Jews as a whole chose to travel on the path of works of the law as the way to righteousness and salvation. It was also learned that there was always a saved Jewish remnant that insured the survival of the nation of Israel even to this day. Israel had missed her Messiah and Paul needs to tell them why, which is still the case today.

> *"He came unto his own, and his own received him not."* (John 1:11)

Lost State Vs. 1-4

1. Brethren, my heart's desire and prayer to God for Israel is, that they might be saved.

2. For I bear them record that they have a zeal for God, but not according to knowledge.

3. For they being ignorant of God's righteousness, and going about to establish their own righteousness, have not submitted themselves unto the righteousness of God.

4. *For Christ is the end of the law for righteousness to everyone that believeth.*

Verse 1 starts with the word brethren, which are the saved souls he is writing to in Rome. He is addressing the Gentiles but is still talking about his kinsmen race. In Romans 9:6 we remember Paul as saying that the word of God was not failing but that the Jews were not being faithful to a faithful God. Israel had possessed religion from Sinai but was not saved. They continue to rebel against God and His Son the Lord Jesus Christ. They had religion and self-righteousness, but not God's righteousness.

This is their very sad condition today which is no different from the unsaved Gentile masses of lost souls. Paul was praying for them to be saved because he knew they could be saved since prayer changes circumstances in people's lives and allows the Holy Ghost to work in sinner's hearts. Besides, Jews are able to receive the gospel just like any Gentile can. The Gentiles in Rome could see that Paul had the same feelings about salvation for them as he had for his kinsmen of Israel.

Paul in Verse 2 addresses the Jews' zeal for God which really translates as a zeal for the law. The Greek for zeal is "zelos" which carries meanings of fervent spirit, ardour in embracing, pursuing or defending something. It contains a fierceness of indignation and is

CHAPTER 3: ROMANS 10

based on feelings and the emotions. All it really is a religious spirit of works to make one feel good that deeds are being done in the name of, in this case, Judaism. Not all zeal is bad.

Phinehas, Aaron's son killed those who worshipped idols, thereby staying God's wrath (numbers 25). But there is zeal that is harmful, is anti-Christ, and is not according to knowledge. This knowledge refers to God's words, on which the Jews' zeal was not being based. Zeal and knowledge must be according to the words of God and not guided by man's thoughts and emotions. Paul was very zealous in pursuit of Christians before he was saved. This was not done in the knowledge of God's words. We as Christians must have feelings and a heart for the lost and a zeal for God's words. Paul had that balance of zeal and knowledge and God wants us to have that also.

Paul states rightly that they, the Jews, have been ignorant of God's righteousness. If you or anybody said that to any Jews today, they would not hold you in very high esteem. But not only the Jews but everybody who rejects Christ today is ignorant of God. Paul accuses the Jews of trying to establish their own righteousness, which is impossible.

The righteousness here in Verse 3 is a legalized self-righteousness. It's the hopeless attempt of man to work out while under the law a character which is approving in God's eyes. This is outside of God's righteousness, and is described as Paul's character by himself:

> "Concerning zeal, persecuting the church; touching the righteousness which is in the law, blameless." (Philippians 3:6)

An unrighteous zeal based on man's knowledge and being under the law can be a very destructive thing.

Verse 4 sums up that Christ finished, fulfilled, and is the end of the law for righteousness. The word for end in the Greek is "Telos", giving the idea of the termination of the present course and a beginning of a new. It is the final end, not destruction on the doing away with, but the conclusion of which the dominion of the law has found in Christ Jesus. Christ is our righteousness to all who are saved for he has fulfilled perfectly all the Law of Moses. There is no going back to it to try to achieve righteousness for there is no longer any righteousness for man under the law.

No Difference Vs. 5-12

> 1. For Moses describeth the righteousness which is of the law, that the man which doeth those things shall live by them.

CHAPTER 3: ROMANS 10

2. But the righteousness which is of faith speaketh on this wise, say not in thine heart, who shall ascent into heaven? (that is, to bring Christ down from above:)
3. Or, who shall descend into the deep? (that is, to bring up Christ again from the dead.)
4. But what saith it? The word is nigh thee, even in thy mouth, and in thy heart: that is, the word of faith, which we preach;
5. That if thou shalt confess with thy mouth the Lord Jesus, and shalt believe in thine heart that God hath raised him from the dead, thou shalt be saved.
6. For with the heart man believeth unto righteousness; and with the mouth confession is made unto salvation.
7. For the scripture saith, whosoever believeth on him shall not be ashamed.
8. For there is no difference between the Jew and the Greek: for the same Lord over all is rich unto all that call upon him.

Leviticus 18:5 says:

"Ye shall therefore keep my statutes, and my judgments: which if a man do, he shall live in them:"

The law was given to Moses for the Israelites to live by. We as faithful servants of Christ Jesus find our righteousness by faith in him. After being justified by his righteousness we please God by faith. Keeping the Law of

Moses has nothing to do with faith and righteousness being imputed.

> *"Knowing that a man is not justified by the works of the law, but by the faith of Jesus Christ, even we have believed in Jesus Christ, that we might be justified by the faith of Christ, and not by the works of the law:"* (Galatians 2:16)

In Verse 6, the words written by Moses under God's inspiration in Deuteronomy 30:11-14 reveal that the Israelites did have the words of God sufficiently available to clearly know and understand the message of salvation. In fact, God was telling the Israelites that availability and accessibility of his words would be there for every generation. That means that God was faithful in supplying His words to Israel in the Old Testament and to the Church in the New Testament. The Jews were told just in Deuteronomy to remember God's words fourteen times and not to forget them another nine times. This exaltation of God's words to us is stated in 2 Peter 12-21. Deuteronomy was written so as to make it understandable to the Israelites what responsibility there was to God. Israel was to receive salvation presented to her by God. They were to take seriously what God was saying, and then turn to Him with all their heart and soul.

CHAPTER 3: ROMANS 10

The Jews, as well as all unsaved people, use the excuse that the words of God are not available or that God is not clear in His intent. But there are many in the world that do not have a Bible or access to one, and so this is another excuse not to believe. Romans 1:18-21 shreds this argument when God says:

> *"For the invisible things of him from the creation of the world are clearly seen, being understood by the things that are made, even his eternal power and Godhead; so that they are without excuse:"* (Romans 1:20)

The words are not hidden, which in the Hebrew is "pala", meaning marvelous or wonderful. It has the meaning that God's words, especially when it comes to being saved, are not so marvelous or so wonderful as to be only in possession of just a few, but can be understood and obeyed by all. They are nigh, or near enough, or close at hand. The close proximity, of God's words is shown by the use of the phrases, even in thy mouth, and in thy heart. As a promise of God, it is repeated in Deuteronomy 30:11-14 to leave man with no argument as to the easy reach of His words by the use of the words mouth and heart. What God has revealed about his salvation by faith is completely sufficient for man to understand, so there is no excuse. Everything that depends upon pleasing God, from a man's point of view, hinges on the closeness of God's words and obeying them. His words are necessary for salvation to every generation, so the promise of God to make available His words to every generation is true.

Paul, in Verse 9, presents what to do in salvation very clearly when we hear the call from Christ. Paul was in the Jewish synagogues all the time preaching Jesus. The word of salvation was covering the Roman Empire and was in the mouths of most people. Salvation by faith was in their ears all the time. Nowadays all that is necessary for a person to be saved from an eternity in hell is to trust in the Gospel of Jesus. He died for our sins and he rose again alive from the grave. The resurrection and the fact that God's power raised him from the dead which confirmed the person and work of Christ, thou shalt be saved. Confession before belief was mentioned by Paul because that was the order mentioned by Moses. Public confession is not to be made before being saved. Faith in Christ is the requirement, faith in Christ's shedding of his blood, faith in His resurrection and standing at the right hand of God being very much alive.

If a person trusts God in his heart, that true faith will be expressed with the mouth in confessing Christ. What is in a person's heart will dictate true confession by faith in the Lord Jesus Christ.

CHAPTER 3: ROMANS 10

In Verse 11, "for the scripture saith", is Isaiah 28:16 being alluded to by Paul.

> *"He that believeth shall not make haste."* (Isa 28:16b).

Paul says, *"shall not be ashamed"*, which is the same thing. Those who believe in the Lord Jesus Christ will not be ashamed. The word haste in Isaiah had the meaning of fear and fleeing because of fear. Many have a fear that believing in Christ will bring such persecution that God will abandon them to their own devices. But whether Jew or Gentile, Christ will never leave us. To the contrary, faith will bring all boldness when Christ be magnified in our bodies is recognized. This, by his Spirit, carries us in life or in death (Philippians 1:20).

Controversy rages over Verse 12 about there being no difference between the Jew and the Greek. This should not be so. The new nature that we receive from Christ at the time of salvation makes no distinction between Jew and Greek.

> *"Even the righteousness of God which is by faith of Jesus Christ unto all and upon all them that believe: for there is no difference:"* (Romans 3:22)

In their flesh there are differences, of course. But saved Jews and saved Gentiles have the same God and are Christians and members of the Church of God. (1 Corinthians

10:32). The Lord is rich unto all that call on him.

> "In whom we have redemption through his blood, the forgiveness of sins, according to the riches of his grace." (Ephesians 1:7)

Whosoever Vs. 13-15

1. For whosoever shall call upon the name of the Lord shall be saved.

2. How then shall the call on him in whom they have not believed? And how shall they believe in him whom they have not heard? And how shall they hear without a preacher?

3. And how shall they preach, except they be sent? As it is written, how beautiful are the feet of them that preach the gospel of peace, and bring glad tidings of good things!

Some have a false notion that Jesus Christ did not die for everyone's sins. But Christ indeed made provision for everybody's sins to be forgiven for whosoever calls upon the Lord. This is a universal offer for anybody in the world, not only for any elect that God may have pre-chosen to be saved. The offer of salvation is only in effect for those who genuinely believe and confess with their mouth in appropriation of the gift.

CHAPTER 3: ROMANS 10

> *"But the gift of God is eternal life through Jesus Christ our Lord." (Romans 6;23b)*
>
> *"That whosoever believeth in him should not perish, but have eternal life." (John 3:15)*

The late pastor Carl Drexler of Runnemede, New Jersey, used to say:

> "Every person in the world has been given the ability of credence (belief). It is available to all."[1]

Verse 14 has the question about how one is able to call on the Savior in whom they have not believed. Paul answers that they have to hear about Christ and who He is and why He had to die.

> *"For he that cometh to God must believe that he is"* (Hebrews 11:6),

That is, that Jesus Christ is our Savior and He has a plan of salvation. Here is Paul, a preacher, among many others, proclaiming the Gospel, and the Jews claimed they never heard of it. But Paul claims that the Jews had plenty of opportunity to receive the word, but the nation did not believe it. They did not believe who Jesus was and denied He even existed. They did not believe the truth, the message was proclaimed so that they could hear, and the messengers of that salvation message were sent by God.

> *"How beautiful upon the mountains are the feet of him that bringeth good tidings, that publisheth peace; that bringeth good tidings of good, that publisheth salvation.* (Isaiah 52:7)

Unfortunately the Jewish people heard the truth about the Messiah and most ignored it. Today a clear presentation of the Gospel is getting out to more of the Jewish people, but much more evangelism is needed.

Israel Rejects Gospel Vs. 16,17

1. *But they have not all obeyed the Gospel. For Esaias saith, Lord, who hath believed our report?*
2. *So then faith cometh by hearing, and hearing by the word of God.*

Israel did not seem to Paul to be very enthusiastic or zealous to receive the good news of the Gospel. Whoever did bring the good news was stoned to death, thrown into prison, brought into the courts. They had killed the prophets, including Stephen, whom Paul himself gave consent to have killed.

Jews were scattered to remote parts of the world at that time and the Gospel was taken by messengers into every nation. As mentioned before, Paul would go into the synagogue in any new city he entered preaching the good news that the Messiah had

CHAPTER 3: ROMANS 10

come. The sad thing is, not many believed the good report.

For Verse 17 the truth is that faith comes from hearing the words of God and we can know the Savior even though we cannot see him. But Israel would not hear, the words of the Gospel fell on deaf ears. Jesus was rejected as the Messiah.

> "He is despised and rejected of men; a man of sorrows, an acquainted with grief: and we did as it were our faces from him: he was despised, and we esteemed him not." (Isaiah 53:3)

The Message Changes Course Vs. 18-21

1. But I say, have they not heard? Yes verily, their sound went into all the earth, and their words unto the ends of the world.

2. But I say, did not Israel know? First Moses saith, I will provoke you to jealousy by them that are no people, and by a foolish nation I will anger you.

3. But Esaias is very bold, and saith, I was found of them that sought me not; I was made manifest unto them that asked not after me.

4. But to Israel he saith, all day long have I stretched forth my hands unto a disobedient and gainsaying people.

In Verse 18, Psalm 19:4 is quoted by Paul.

> "Their line is gone out through all the earth, and their words to the end of the world."

It is alluded to that the words of the Gospel have gone forth to the ends of the world before there were preachers. The revelation of God and his salvation through his glorious Son, Jesus Christ, resonated through the created universe. The general revelation of God's creation should have been heard by all the earth. The special revelation of God has gone forth by his Hebrew, Aramaic, and Greek his Hebrew, Aramaic, and Greek words contained in our King James Bible. Israel knew because of the sounds and the words had reached to them.

Verse 19 asks did Israel know the Gospel? They rejected the words and the Word of God, the Lord Jesus Christ. Paul recorded what he discovered after dealing with the Jews:

> "In the heart of this people is waxed gross, and their ears are dull of hearing, and their eyes have they closed; (Acts 28:27a)

The Jews knew all the Scriptures, they even had the Savior preach to them for three years. They had the Prophets, they had the words of God written down. Finally they were told that God was going to find Himself a new people and that Israel was to be jolted into jealousy.

CHAPTER 3: ROMANS 10

Moses had already prophesied such an event.

> *"And I will move them to jealousy with those which are not a people: I will provoke them to anger with a foolish nation."* (Deuteronomy 32:21b)

The Jews, unfortunately, did not believe God would do that to them, but he did. The Jews snubbed God and the heathen were brought close to God by belief in the Gospel. The heathen up to that point were shut out and had no hope of salvation. This completely changed because God sent Paul to the Gentiles to take out a people for Himself and build his Church. The Jews got angry and are still angry because God had laid them aside temporarily.

> *"Be it known therefore unto you, that the salvation of God is sent unto the Gentiles, and that they will hear it."* (Acts 28:28)

In Verse 20 it says that the Gentiles were not looking for salvation, they cared not for the things of God.

> *"I am sought of them that asked not for me; I am found of them that sought me not;"* (Isaiah 65:1a)

There were a few exceptions in the Old Testament, but when the Lord opened the door for Paul to take the Gospel to the Gentiles, that is when the Church grew and grew.

> *"He came unto his own, and his own received him not."* (John 1:11)

Jesus Christ came only to the house of Israel. There was no Church yet when Jesus was on earth. After Christ rose from the dead the Church started with Jewish converts. When Paul took the Gospel to the Gentiles, the Church grew and spread.

> *"But as many as received him, to them gave he power to become the sons of God, even to them that believe on his name:"* (John 1:12)

In Verse 21 God turns his attention one final time to his beloved Israel. Quoting from Isaiah 65:2:

> *"I have spread out my hands all the day unto a rebellious people, which walketh in a way that was not good, after their own thoughts:"*

Israel's problem was her stubborn disobedience. Paul calls them a gainsaying people. Gainsaying has the meaning of contradicting, to deny, oppose, disobey, revile, and to speak against. They finally got to the point that they wanted nothing to do with the Lord and became totally rebellious. All this time, even at this moment, the Lord's hands are stretched out to Israel, pleading with them to trust him.

Chapter 4

Romans 11

I, Paul: Vs. 1

> *I say then, hath God cast away his people? God forbid. For I also am an Israelite, of the seed of Abraham, of the tribe of Benjamin.*

Israel has not been forever set aside or cast off for good and left to die is the theme of this chapter. God is not done with Israel, his chosen people, for he has a future for them. Paul's salvation proves that there is a remnant, in his time, as well as in the present.

> *"For the Lord will not cast off his people,...but judgment shall return unto righteousness:"* (Psalm 94:14a, 15a)

Israel is judged for its rejection and disobedience to God. Judgment will return righteousness among the Jews in the future. God will never cast off his people of Israel. There are those who teach that God is finished with Israel and that Israel has now become the Church. But as Paul was preaching, the Jews were only a few short years away from being scattered throughout the world for the next 1900 years. But it was prophesied that Israel would become a nation again in the latter days.

> *"Therefore will he give them up, until the time that she which travaileth hath brought forth: then the remnant of his brethren shall return unto the children of Israel."* (Micah 5:3)

Israel was not only to be re-gathered as a nation again, it was to be brought forth in one day, at once. This prophecy was fulfilled on May 14, 1948.

> *"Who hath heard such a thing? Who hath seen such things? Shall the earth be made to bring forth in one day? Or shall a nation be born at once? For as soon as Zion travailed, she brought forth her children."* (Isaiah 66:8)

David Ben-Gurion announced, "The state of Israel is established." The next morning Israel came under attack from Egyptian, Syrian, Lebanese, Jordanian, and Iraqi forces.

There are even further prophesies about Israel:

> *"After this I will return, and will build again the tabernacle of David, which is fallen down: And I will build again the ruins thereof, and I will set it up:"* (Acts 15:16)

Christ will return to rebuild the tabernacle of David, which is in ruins today.

CHAPTER 4: ROMANS 11

Paul was an Israelite, a Jew descendant from Abraham, and born of the tribe Benjamin. God will again bless and dwell with his people, who are the offspring of Jacob through his twelve sons. Paul was not cast away. God saved Paul, as he would save every Jew who would turn to him. King Saul, his son Jonathan, Esther, and Mordecai were all Benjamites. The tribe of Benjamin was highly respected and honored by all Jews, even to this day. This bolsters Paul's argument that God is not finished with Israel. Paul was in line to reject God before his conversion.

> "Who was before a blasphemer, and a persecutor, and injurious, but I obtained mercy," (1 Timothy 1:13)

If total rejection of Israel was the plan God had for them, he would not have bothered to save the greatest Christ-rejecting Jew there was. God is not done with the Jewish Christ-rejectors and Paul was proof as well as a remnant of Bible believing Jews that are saved today.

The Saved remnant Vs. 2-6

1. *God hath not cast away his people which he foreknew. Wot ye not what the scripture saith of Elias? How he maketh intercession to God against Israel, saying,*

2. *Lord, they have killed thy prophets, and digged down thine altars, and I am left alone, and they seek my life.*

3. But what saith the answer of God unto him? I have reserved to myself seven thousand men, who have not bowed the knee to the image of Baal.

4. Even so then at the present time there is a remnant according to the election of grace.

5. And if by grace, then is it no more of works: but if it be of works, then is it no more grace: otherwise work is no more work.

God very strongly states in Verse 2 that he has not cast away his people from any future considerations. His people trace from the Old Testament times and by calling them His people, God singles them out as unique and special to Him. He knew what their past, present, and future would be ahead of time. God looked down through time and chose Abraham to be the father of his chosen people. Then Elijah is mentioned making his prayer to God to come down hard on Israel for their wickedness and idolatry. Elijah cried to the Lord:

> "For the children of Israel have forsaken thy covenant, thrown down thin altars, and slain thy prophets with the sword; and I, even I only, am left; and they seek my life, to take it away." (1 Kings 19:10)

Paul is quoting this scripture from 1 Kings to show that God will never cast away his people, even when they turned from him to worthless gods and idols. The evil Jezebel had

CHAPTER 4: ROMANS 11

made Baal worship the official religion of Israel. Elijah wanted judgment to come upon Israel. This was after Jezebel had threatened to kill Elijah the next day. What went through Elijah's head is called the Elijah complex today. He let Satan magnify the situation so much that Elijah lost sight of God. He fled to a cave where the Lord met him. But Elijah thought he was all alone and the only righteous prophet against all the prophets of Baal. He wanted to die, *"It is enough; now, O Lord, take away my life;"* (1Kings 19:4b). It was just the day before that God had given Elijah the victory over the prophets of Baal at the altars. But terror had gripped him and he was blinded by his seemingly hopeless situation. On top of that was his sinful pride in thinking he was the only prophet left and he wanted to be done away with.

In Verse 4 God had an answer for Elijah. It was God's way to preserve Israel when everything seemed hopeless and Satan had finally managed to wipe out Israel. When the Lord appeared to him he gave his lament for a second time that he alone was left and there was a price on his head. But the Lord reassured Elijah that he was in control and that he had the preservation of Israel all under control. He was to go and anoint Hazael king over Syria. Then he was to anoint Jehu king over Israel. Elisha was to be anointed the next prophet in Elijah's place. Oh, and by the way, the Lord to Elijah:

> *"Yet I have left me seven thousand in Israel, all the knees which have not bowed unto Baal, and every mouth which hath not kissed him."* (1 Kings 19:18)

We feel that we are alone at times when we hold closely to all the doctrines of the Bible. Amongst great apostasy, compromise, false religions, cults, Islam, etc., etc., we feel as though we are alone. It is with that still, small, voice that God will reveal His never dying love for us and a remnant will always be there. There are many standing and we need to stand with them.

Paul was saying in Verse 5 that there was a remnant of Jews that were believers then and there are many who form the saved remnant now. God's election of grace chose them to know Him then and that grace is the same today. There will come a time when God will raise up Israel as a nation to Him. They will gaze on Him whom they have pierced (Zechariah 12:10). Paul is talking about just a remnant back then. Just as the chosen remnant in Elijah's time kept the Lord from casting off Israel, the remnant in Paul's day accomplished the same result. The remnant that Paul was talking about was another proof that God had not cast away the nation of Israel.

In Verse 6 Paul talks about the remnant believing by the election of grace. The majority of Israel was trying to earn God's favor by doing good works according to the law. But if a believer is saved by grace it is not through works. This Jewish remnant trusts in God's grace. They have faith, and faith is not a work as some teach. If someone does not believe by faith through grace, he cannot reach salvation by works. If you could obtain by works then it is no longer God's grace. Grace and works are separate, complete opposites.

Israel is Blind   Vs. 7-10

1. *What then? Israel hath not obtained that which he seeketh for; but the election hath obtained it, and the rest were blinded.*

2. *(According as it is written, God hath given them the spirit of slumber, eyes that they should not see, and ears that they should not hear;) unto this day.*

3. *And David saith, let their table be made a snare, and a trap, and a stumbling block, and a recompence unto them:*

4. *Let their eyes be darkened, that they may not see, and bow down their back alway.*

In Verse 7 Paul is stating Israel's spiritual condition. Israel was a country of seekers. The work seek is from the Greek "epizeteo", and describes seeking to acquire or obtain something, strive after, long for earnestly. There is an element of persistency to the Israelites seeking after righteousness but failed due to going about it by works. Israel, as a nation, did not attain the blessing they sought but the chosen portion of them had obtained.

> *"For the preaching of the cross is to them that perish foolishness; but unto us which are saved it is the power of God."* (1 Corinthians 1:18)

Israel had not attained unto grace, therefore as a result of their doctrine of works unto righteousness their hearts were hardened, or blinded. The Greek word is "poroo", and it means to harden, make hard like a stone, to be callous and insensitive. The national Jews had become spiritually hardened to the Gospel, and blinded to God's tender reaching out to them. The Jews were insensitive to the teaching and the truth, before when Jesus spoke with them, and now as Paul is speaking to them. This blindness affects the understanding as well as the heart. In Romans 9:18 God says that he will have mercy on those he will have mercy and whom he will harden. In respect to Pharaoh it is written that God hardened Pharaoh's heart eleven times and Pharaoh hardened his own heart three times. We may assume that God hardened the Jews and as a result of their

CHAPTER 4: ROMANS 11

further hardening God judicially hardened them so that those who were not saved could not believe the truth. Either way, the spiritual state of those blinded is very dire. To be abandoned by God to the hardness of your heart is very, very serious.

Verse 8 begins with *"as it is written"* which is the Greek future tense which means the Hebrew, Aramaic, and Greek words of scripture were preserved from the past, up to the present, and on into the future. Israel had been given this blindness a very long time ago.

> *"Yet the Lord hath not given you a heart to perceive, and eyes to see, and ears to hear, unto this day." (Deuteronomy 29:4)*

> *"They have not known nor understood. For he hath shut their eyes, that they cannot see, and their hearts, that they cannot understand."* (Isaiah 44:18)

The purpose of Paul is still to prove that Israel's history of rejection and hardness has not resulted in God's permanently setting them aside. Their rejection of the Messiah in Paul's time coincides with this. They physically beheld the Messiah in their midst and could not recognize him they were so blind. This blindness and hardness exists today and Israel in the land is not saved. But the Lord will be praised for that day will come that after the Tribulation the blindness will be lifted and those left standing will look upon the Lord Jesus Christ whom they have pierced and mourn for him.

> *"And they shall look upon me whom they have pierced, and they shall mourn for him."* (Zechariah 12:10b)

Paul continues in Verse 9 what God had done in the past to deal with Israel's unbelief and rejection. Paul quotes David in the great suffering Psalm 69. The imprecatory Verse 22 lists their table as being a snare, a trap, and a stumbling block. The table refers to the Passover which looked forward to Calvary and their Messiah. Jesus Christ was the Passover Lamb who was looked for since that first Passover in Egypt. But Israel was blinded with darkened eyes as the Lord Jesus hung on the Cross. The fear of that first Passover night as the killing angel went forth is still upon Israel. The Table of Israel, the Passover has become a snare to Israel even up to today. By continuing to observe Passover every year, it is a snare and a trap and a stumbling block to them since they keep looking forward for the Messiah, the blessing that was to be conferred upon Jews from observing the Passover has become a curse.

Verse 10 forcibly expresses the cursedness of hardness through the dimming of vision and discrepancy of a bowed back that is seen in old age. This is such a clear example of the just and certain judgments of God. David prayed to God to let them be treated so, and Paul points out to the Jews that it is true that they suffered these very judgments. The Jews of Paul's day became so hardened that they could not see that these things had already been experienced all along their history and the same were predicted for them in the prophets.

So, the conversion of Paul, a Pharisee, the identity of the chosen remnant, and Israel's hardened condition, all prove that God has not cast away his people.

God's Purposes Declared   Vs. 11-12

1. *I say then, have they stumbled that they should fall? God forbid: but rather through their fall salvation is come unto the Gentiles, for to provoke them to jealousy.*
2. *Now if the fall of them be the riches of the world, and the diminishing of them the riches of the Gentiles; how much more their fullness?*

Paul is addressing the salvation of the Gentiles by God's sovereignty in V11. Just like in 11:1 Paul uses the same approach, I say then..., to again punctuate that because the Jews had rejected God, His rejection of His people would be temporary and not final. They had not fallen so far as to be hopeless beyond God's saving hand. By their being set aside for the time being, facilitation to the Gospel is being preached to the Gentiles. Jesus had predicted this and told the Israelites in Matthew 21:43, but they did not believe him. Their stumbling enabled God to save Gentiles which for the Jews would instill jealousy since the Gentiles would be enjoying the blessings of salvation that they were working so hard to achieve on their own. It should have moved the Jews to imitate the Christians onto the path of true righteousness through faith, instead of jealousy.

It, the salvation of the Gentiles, was meant to bring about the restoration of Israel by provoking them. By the day of Pentecost God's program was for calling out a Jewish remnant and large numbers of Gentiles to build his church. For these 2000 years of God's building His Church shows God's sovereignty in fulfilling his purposes.

Provoking the Jews and saving Gentiles is all leading to the day when Israel will finally see that the Gentiles indeed are following the Messiah. This will provoke them into embracing Jesus Christ as Messiah. Using the fall of Israel to bless the whole world is also part of God's purpose.

Verse 12 looks forward to the Millennial Kingdom. God is not dealing with Israel as a nation at this time, but extending the Gospel

CHAPTER 4: ROMANS 11

to individual Jews to salvation. It will be a different world in the time God picks up again with his chosen nation. This verse is talking to the riches in store for the whole world, which will be some Gentile nations, after God restores Israel to her position of head of all nations. Israel will be given full blessings and fulfillment of God's promises to them in the future. There will be a future for Israel. But because they have been set aside for now, the riches of the Lord's blessings could begin to fall on the Gentiles. This is a verse that the Replacement Theologists do not accept. Christians experience some blessings now, being the temple of the Holy Ghost and is assured of an inheritance with Jesus Christ in heavenly places. A Christian can go directly to God seeking supplications. Peace, joy, and other fruits of the Spirit bless the Christian. When Israel is restored in the Kingdom, they will enjoy the fullness of blessings. How much more in the Millennium that the Gentiles will be blessed through Israel? It will be glorious for Israel and all the nations when Christ personally reigns on the throne of David in Jerusalem. There will be a different world when the blinders will be taken off.

> "at that time the curse will be lifted, paradise will be regained, the animal kingdom will be at peace, the Lord will reign out of Jerusalem, the Old Testament Saints will be resurrected, the Shekinah

glory will once again fill the temple, Satan will be bound, Israel and the Church will reign with Christ, and peace, joy, and righteousness will prevail."[1]

Purposes of God Proven Vs. 13-15

1. *For I speak to you Gentiles, inasmuch as I am the apostle of the Gentiles, I magnify mine office;*
2. *If by any means I may provoke to emulation them which are my flesh, and might save some of them.*
3. *For if the casting away of them be the reconciling of the world, what shall the receiving of them be, but life from the dead?*

Paul is challenging those who may have been confused as to his true intentions in ministry. Here he was been so concerned about the Jews hearing the Gospel and how God was going to be blessing them in the Kingdom. He says to the Gentiles that he is the sent apostle to them and that God's purposes would be fulfilled. God intended to send him to the Gentiles but allowed Paul to approach his kinsmen all that was on his heart.

> *"For he is a chosen vessel unto me, to bear my name before the gentiles, and kings, and the children of Israel."* (Acts 9:15)

Paul found himself explaining his ministry to the Gentiles around him. He was concerned

CHAPTER 4: ROMANS 11

about the hardened Israelites, but his main ministry was still to the Gentiles. Peter was the apostle to the Jews. But Paul considered it glorious that some Jews were saved through his ministry and gave that glory to God. Paul took the Gospel mainly to the unsaved Gentiles for he saw that the Jewish people would see that they also needed to be saved.

Verse 14 continues the thought that Paul coveted Gentile converts to Jesus. It was constantly on his mind to provoke his fellow Jews according to the flesh to follow the Gentiles to be saved. To Paul it made no difference who was to be saved, just so he could save some Jews. Paul wanted Jews to be stirred by the spiritual blessings in Gentiles to motivate Jews to come to Jesus. The Jews spent much time and energy doing good works and they knew they weren't getting anywhere with God. It is the same way today. We must be like Paul and inspire Jews to emulate us by being spiritually attractive to them. They are frustrated and we as Christians together with the words of God are the answer to Jewish salvation. They see peace, joy, faith, satisfaction in Jesus, purpose, and love in us, they will be moved to jealousy. Gentile believers make the most impression on Jews. It would be good for Gentile Christians to be the best they can to the unsaved Jewish community. They need to perceive Gentile believers possess quality, spirit-filled lives worth emulating.

Verse 15 starts with the phrase, if the casting away of them. Paul is talking still that God is not permanently through with Israel yet and never intended to be. The purpose of God for setting aide Israel would be for the reconciliation of those who had no hope of being brought close to God were joined to Him by the blood of Christ. God had gone to the Israelites with the salvation message. Very few outside of Israel were brought into a relationship with God. So if Israel was not moved out of the way, the Gentiles would never have heard the good news as Paul took the Gospel to Asia Minor and Europe to evangelize.

On the other side of the coin, Paul contrasts this sentiment of Israel, being saved and the world being blessed during the millennial kingdom. Paul is looking forward to the time Israel will be reborn, regenerated, and will be the head and not the tail, but the leader of all nations.

Principle of Israel's Restoration Vs. 16-22

1. *For if the first fruit be holy, the lump is also holy: and if the root be holy, so are the branches.*

CHAPTER 4: ROMANS 11

> 2. And if some of the branches be broken off, and thou, being a wild olive tree, wert graffed in among them, and with them partakest of the root and fatness of the olive tree;
>
> 3. Boast not against the branches, but if thou boast, thou bearest not the root, but the root thee.
>
> 4. Thou wilt say then, the branches were broken off, that I might be graffed in.
>
> 5. Well; because of unbelief they were broken off, and thou standest by faith. Be not high minded, but fear:
>
> 6. For if God spared not the natural branches, take heed lest he also spare not thee.
>
> 7. Behold therefore the goodness and severity of God: on them which fell, severity; but toward thee, goodness, if thou continue in his goodness: otherwise thou also shalt be cut off.

The word first fruit in Verse 16 is the key to understanding the verse. This section is key for Gentiles to have a proper perspective of Israel's restoration and understanding of God's grace. First fruit is an analogy to the dough in the Mosaic Law. It was to be part of the Feast of First Fruits that the first and best part of the harvest was to be waved unto the Lord Jesus Christ who became the first fruit on being resurrected from the dead. The first fruit of the dough offering and of the harvest looked forward to the resurrection of the Lord

Jesus Christ. Paul told the Jews that they needed to believe that Christ was raised from the dead to be saved.

> *"That if thou shalt confess with thy mouth the Lord Jesus, and shalt believe in thine heart that God hath raised him from the dead, thou shalt be saved."* (Romans 10:9)

Paul was relating the resurrection to first fruits, since the Jews would understand what was happening. The body of Jesus that was dead, just like the seed, could live and did live again. His body was planted in the earth and was waved again the third day.[2]

The first fruit was holy or set aside to the Lord. Holy is from the Greek, "Hagios", which means set apart, sanctified, consecrated. Paul is saying then, that the first fruit, the resurrected Christ is holy or set apart.

> *"But now is Christ risen from the dead, and become the first fruits of them that slept."* (1 Corinthians 15:20).

If a part of the dough, according to Mosaic Law (Numbers 15:18-21), was given to the Lord, via the priest, it was symbolic that the whole lump belonged to God. Lump is from the Greek, "phurama", the same word Paul used (Romans 9:21) to describe the potter's lump to describe the lost nation of Israel.

CHAPTER 4: ROMANS 11

The root and branches are a parallel usage of Christ and the olive tree of Israel. If the root of the tree, Christ, be consecrated and holy unto God, then the branches (Israel) are also set apart to him. This was true as long as the atoning sacrifices were still acceptable unto God.

These analogies Paul is giving are the basis of God's restoring a rejected nation of Israel back to her place of privilege. The root and tree, which is Christ symbolically, shows that the holy branches were in a place of blessing which stemmed from the unconditional covenant made by God with Abraham. The lump and branches represent the Jewish people. Israel has stumbled but it is only temporary until her inevitable restoration.

Paul says in Verse 17 that the branches representing unsaved, National Israel have been broken off temporarily. There were still some remnant, saved Jews, branches partaking of the root, but the unbelieving branches had been cut off. This coincides with verse 11 in the words, "they should fall?" Therefore, some of the branches remained and God took other branches from a wild olive tree to graft in among them. These, of course, are the saved Gentiles from the time of the start of the Great Commission until now. This term, wild olive tree, "agrielaios", is only found here and in Verse 24. The word, thou, in this verse links it to the saved Gentiles to whom Paul was speaking. These two groups of believers are both partaking of the spiritual blessings that come from the covenant of Abraham.

Verse 18 says that the saved Gentiles, wild branches, were not to boast against unbelieving Jews who are not enjoying the spiritual privileges. This is called spiritual pride where Gentiles can think of themselves as better than the Jews. This is true when it comes to supersessionism in the church. Some believe that the Jews have been cast off for good and the church is the replacement for Israel with all of its promises being appropriated.

Christians are not to look down on unbelieving Jews. They are to set an example of the redeemed life before them in humility, the opposite of pride. Pride comes naturally for the sinful nature within man, and we must always guard our hearts through Jesus Christ against it. There is nothing to boast of since the salvation being extended to the Gentiles was brought about by the fall of the Jews. We are to pray for Jews so that they may be saved. Give them the Gospel and have the perspective that someday they will be grafted back in again. We are reminded that it is the Lord Jesus Christ, the root, that holds us by faith, so we must not allow hatred and pride any space.

CHAPTER 4: ROMANS 11

Verse 19 reminds us again that it was because of Israel's downfall, that Gentiles are grafted into the tree which is Christ. The natural branches that are left in are the chosen people. The unbelieving Jews have been broken off. They must be given the Gospel, even though they deny Jesus Christ is the Messiah. We are not to despise the Jews. The chosen people now include the Church, the true believers in the Lord Jesus Christ. All this has happened through the mercy, love, and righteousness of God.

Verse 20 states that Israel was broken off for the sole reason of unbelief in the Lord Jesus Christ as the Messiah. Paul had to remind the Christians that they stood before God by faith. Evidently the Christians of Paul's time were taking on a superiority attitude over those unbelieving Jews. They may have been fostering a replacement type of thinking towards the Jews, and this has very bad consequences. They may have been imitating past Jewish bigotries. At times Jews thought that God could only have a privileged relationship with the Jews and never a Gentile.

Christians are to guard against ever being high-minded. The Greek word for high-minded is, "hupselophroneo." This is to be proud or arrogant. This is thinking that one is great, or somebody to be reckoned with. Everything is going just great, but God says to hold on, be a little humble. Have some fear. The Christian is to remember who God is and not let the sin of pride bring God's chastisement and correction to us. The Christians in Rome were developing pride in their hearts toward unsaved Jews, or all people, and God is commanding them to stop immediately. This would be the wise thing for Christians to do today if they are guilty of the same sin.

> "Wherefore let him that thinketh he standeth take heed lest he fall." (1 Corinthians 10:12)

Verse 21 is another warning to those who stand by faith. God at the first took great pains to establish a chosen people for Himself. God called Abraham and the other fathers of Israel. The people of Israel and the fathers were the natural branches. God loved them dearly as his chosen people. But God did not spare the natural branches after so many centuries of rejecting Him, but their unbelief caused God to spare not even his chosen. Those who are saved are in the Lord Jesus Christ. This is a larger warning to our country as well as others who are choosing their own way, apart from God. God will save remnants from every country, but he will cut off those who reject him and His Son, just like he had done to Israel. "Why should God have any

CHAPTER 4: ROMANS 11

more regard for a faithless Gentile Christianity, than for faithless Judasim?[3]

Verse 22 gives another warning to the Christians at Rome and elsewhere. Just because Christians have security in their salvation, the Roman Church, as did others, did not heed God's words and relied more and more on their works. This Roman Church of Paul was swallowed up by the Roman Catholic Church which mixes works and a false graces Gospel. This Roman Catholicism is present today and ecumenically is leading a global liberal apostate church. It claims to be Christian but denies the Deity of Christ, attacks the pure works of the Bible, and prevents the true Gospel to go out to the lost. The early churches walked by works and not by faith. Along with the natural branches of Israel, they suffered the severity of God. The goodness of God fell on the Gentiles, but they fell along the way, with only remnants today left to grow in God's grace. This harkens back to Romans 9:6 where Paul says, "For they are not all Israel, which are of Israel." This carries to today when it can be said that not all of Christendom is of the Church.

The fact exists with God that the false Gentile church can be cut off for unbelief, as it is also possible for Israel to be grafted back in for believing the Gospel.

Possible Restoration Vs. 23-24

1. *And they also, if they abide not still in unbelief, shall be graffed in. For God is able to graff them in again.*
2. *For if thou wert cut out of the olive tree which is wild by nature, and wert graffed contrary to nature into a good olive tree: how much more shall these, which be the natural branches, be graffed into their own olive tree?*

Verses 23 and 24 demonstrate God's mercy for Paul is stating the possibility for Israel to receive Christ in the future. He holds out the promise that Israel would be grafted back into the olive tree once again. There are only a few saved Jews today and they make up the remnant. If the rest of Israel ever wants what was given to the Gentiles, then God is willing, able, and waiting to graft them back in.

Verse 24 says that the Gentiles were the wild olive tree that was grafted into the good olive tree, which is contrary to what goes on in nature. Observe.

Ever since Bible times it was common to graft olive trees. A branch from a good, very fruitful olive tree was grafted onto a wild olive tree. The wild olive tree would produce sparse, small fruit not containing much oil. A good cultivated tree produced the very good

CHAPTER 4: ROMANS 11

growing, oil producing olives. Several cultivated olive tree branches were grafted onto a wild olive tree. As we read in Romans 11:17, God grafted wild olive tree branches signifying the Gentiles, into the good olive tree, since the unbelieving, natural branches were broken off.

This was the opposite way of grafting back then, and contrary to nature. Paul was saying that God was grafting the wild into the good, not the good into the wild. It's true that if you graft the good into the wild, the cultivated will win out, but the opposite is never true. If you graft a wild branch of anything into a good, cultivated tree, the wild will take over. God makes his grafting by grace, so it has to work. Paul was showing God's magnified mercy being shown to the Gentiles by grafting such a wild, pagan race into the good olive tree.

As God said previously, the Gentiles need not be filled with boastful pride over the unbelieving Jewish state. He went to all the trouble to bend nature's rules to do an unnatural merciful thing to bring salvation to the Gentiles. If God was willing and able to do that, he can more easily graft the natural branches back into their own olive tree. Faith is the key to the Jewish Nation's future. To be restored to their place in God depends on belief in the Lord Jesus Christ as their Messiah.

All the possibilities and promises indicate a glory-filled future for Israel.

The Promise of Restoration   Vs. 25-29

1. *For I would not, brethren, that ye should be ignorant of this mystery, lest ye should be wise in your own conceits; that blindness in pat is happened to Israel, until the fulness of the Gentiles be come in.*

2. *And so all Israel shall be saved; as it is written, there shall come out of Sion the Deliverer, and shall turn away ungodliness from Jacob:*

3. *For this is my covenant unto them, when I shall take away their sins.*

4. *As concerning the Gospel, they are enemies for your sakes: but as touching the election, they are beloved for the Father's sakes.*

5. *For the gifts and calling of God are without repentance.*

Verse 25 finds Paul talking still to the brethren, the saved, in Rome. We just read about the miracle of God grafting the church into the good olive tree of spiritual blessings. So, there is no difference between a saved Jew and a saved Gentile. Here, Paul is talking about the mystery of that blindness that has happened to Israel being lifted. In Biblical terms, a mystery is something that has been

CHAPTER 4: ROMANS 11

hidden in God's mind, but is now revealed by new information for the first time.

> *"(as I wrote afore in few words, whereby, when ye read, ye may understand my knowledge in the mystery of Christ)."* (Ephesians 3:3b,4)

Again, the apostle warns these Roman Christians not to be wise in this matter, or keep acting like they know everything. There are many today who think they know everything, but God calls them, "wise in their own conceit." Beware of becoming conceited, another prideful sin.

The mystery revealed is that the blindness to Israel in part will be lifted when the fullness of the Gentiles is ended. The blindness was only in part to Israel. This was known. There would be a saved remnant of Israelites in each generation. The total amount of time that the hardness of Israel would last had been hidden by God. Through the ages, since the day of Pentecost, Jews were able to escape the hardening that was upon Israel, to enter into the Church along with the Gentiles.

The understanding of the new information in this verse, hinges on the phrase, *"until the fulness of the Gentiles be come in."* The Gentiles are ruling countries today, where that position will be reversed in the Kingdom. Jesus said:

> *"And Jerusalem shall be trodden down of the Gentiles, until the times of the Gentiles be fulfilled."* (Luke 21:24b)

This verse refers to the siege by Titus in 70 A.D. when the city was taken and this prophecy was literally fulfilled. This scene foreshadows vaguely the final siege at the end of this age, post-rapture by thee and a half years, when the city will be taken. Matthew 24 and Mark 13 portray the Tribulation siege itself.

The ending of the unbelief in Israel and the fullness of the Gentiles are future events and the former is dependent on the latter. The common accepted interpretation of the fullness of the Gentiles is that it happens at the rapture, when the last member of the Church is added making it complete. There are reasons that this could not be. There is no real indication that scripture says that Israel awakens to the truth of the Messiah at the rapture. Their unbelief is lifted at the time of Jacob's trouble, in the latter half of the Tribulation. As was mentioned in vs 23 and 24 God had cut off Israel because of unbelief, liberalism, and apostasy. God alludes to the same thing as having the power to cut off Gentile nations that reject the Lord Jesus Christ and grafting Israel back in. That time is nearing soon, as the apostle has continued the discussion to the fullness of the Gentiles in Verse 25.

> *"I will heal their backsliding, I will love them freely: for mine anger is turned away from him."* (Hosea 14:4).

> *"His branches shall spread, and his beauty shall be as the olive tree, and his smell as Lebanon."* (Hosea 14:6).

The cutting off of the Gentiles would be as Daniel describes:

> *"Thou sawest till that a stone was cut out without hands, which smoke the image upon his feet that were of iron and clay, and break them to pieces."* (Daniel 2:34)

The fullness of Israel in Romans 11:12 is the bringing in of the Kingdom, the Kingdom where Christ is King and Israel will be the head of nations. Thus the fullness of the Gentiles refers to the worldwide Beast Kingdom, the goal of Satan, the pinnacle of Gentile power and rule. This fullness Beast Kingdom of the Gentiles will give way to the fullness of Israel.

Thus the fullness of the Gentiles is the formation of the Tribulation global government of the Beast, and its supreme ruler the anti-Christ. The anti-Christ system will not stand based on Paul's doctrine stated in Verse 20. The governing by unbelief and not by faith will be cut off. Godless empires may rise up, but none can stand.

Verse 26 is a popular verse for controversy and disagreement among some Christians. Having established the fact that Israel's blindness will begin to end at the abomination of desolation and then completely at the cutting off of the last Gentile Empire, the Lord Jesus Christ returns to deliver Israel and set up His Kingdom.

> *"Two parts therein shall be cut off and die; but the third shall be left therein...And I will bring the third part,...they shall call on my name, and I will hear them: I will say, It is my people:"* (Zechariah 13: 8.9)

Two-thirds of the Jews will be killed during the Tribulation. One third of the population will be saved. There are approximately 9 million Jews is Israel as of 2014. If the Tribulation was to start today 5.3 million Jews will be killed by the Anti-Christ, and 2.7 million will call on the Lord Jesus and be saved by receiving him as Lord and Savior.

It is during the week the seven year peace treaty is signed with Israel, that the Anti-Christ will establish his kingdom, and allow the Jews to live secured in their borders. Three and one-half years, in a permitted place of worship near the Dome of the Rock, the Anti-Christ will break the treaty, offer the abomination in their temple, and move to kill all the Jews that do not honor him as the Messiah. They will escape, "then let them

CHAPTER 4: ROMANS 11

which be in Judea flee into the mountains," to the southeast of Jerusalem, most likely to a hiding place called Petra.

This Tribulation remnant of Jews will be hidden and protected by the Lord.

> "and to the woman were given two wings of a great eagle, that she may fly into the wilderness, into her place, where she is nourished for a time, and times, and half a time, from the face of the serpent." (Revelation 12:14)

This harkens back to when the Lord when he brought the Israelites from Egypt to Sinai by grace.

> "ye have seen what I did unto the Egyptians, and how I bare you on eagle's wings, and brought you unto myself." (Exodus 19:4)

Then we read of the deliverer out of Sion, the Lord who will appear when the armies of Anti-Christ are destroyed, and will return for Israel and the start of the Millennium.

> "The Lord also shall roar out of Zion, and utter his voice from Jerusalem;" (Joel 3:16a)

> "And I will pour upon the house of David, and upon the inhabitants of Jerusalem, the spirit of grace and of supplications, and they shall look upon me whom they have pierced, and they shall

> mourn for him...and shall be in bitterness for him." (Zechariah 12:10)

When the Jews see their deliverer they will know him by His pierced hands, feet, and side, and will know that it is the Messiah, the Lord Jesus Christ. They will mourn very bitterly and shall all Israel be saved. This is based on the promise of God to take away the sins of Israel.

> "Seventy weeks are determined upon thy people and upon thy holy city, to finish the transgression, and to make an end to sins,..." (Daniel 9:24)

When Israel does accept the Lord Jesus Christ as their Messiah, all 2.7 million, then all Israel will be saved and their sins and reproach will be taken away and the kingdom brought in.

Verse 27 tells us that it was God's covenant, or agreement with them, the Israelites, that He would take away their sins. Isaiah 59:21 tells us that, "this is my covenant with them,"

God will make a new covenant with the redeemed Tribulation Israel.

> "Behold, the days come, saith the Lord, that I will make a new covenant with the house of Israel, and with the house of Judah," (Jeremiah 31:31)

God's law will be written by God in their hearts. Every person in Israel under the new

CHAPTER 4: ROMANS 11

covenant will know God and his words in his heart, there will be no ignorance of God's words.

> *"for I will forgive their iniquity, and I will remember their sin no more."* (Jeremiah 31:34b)

This will be all Israel that which are of Israel, and Paul started discussion about in Romans 9:6. This is the defense in full of God's righteousness in his dealings with Israel.

Verse 28 returns to the present age of grace according to the Gospel commission. Paul recounts that the Jews had rejected the Gospel and God defines them as enemies of the Gospel. Gentiles need to realize that because of their unbelief and rejection of Jesus Christ as the Messiah, Israel has stumbled and been set aside to allow Gentiles a chance to hear and believe and be saved.

But, Paul warns believers, that God has chosen the Jews as his beloved even though they are not all Israel. They are beloved for the fathers' sakes. The fathers mentioned here are Abraham, Isaac, and Jacob and the promises by God to them for the future restoration of Israel.

We know that God's purposes for Israel will be fulfilled in spite of their hardness, according to Verse 29. Gentiles have no reason to boast of their spiritual fortune at the expense of the

Jews. Many, many Gentiles have been saved as a result. God will not change his mind about the gifts and calling of God are irretractable. God will make Israel a blessed nation, calling Israel into being a nation, and bestowing multiple gifts on her.

The Mercies of God Vs. 30-32

1. *For as ye in times past have not believed God, yet have not obtained mercy through their unbelief:*

2. *Even so have these also now not believed, that through your mercy they also may obtain mercy.*

3. *For God hath concluded them all in unbelief, that he might have mercy on them all.*

Paul, in Verse 30, in talking to the saved Gentiles talks about a future time when Israel will finally understand the mercy of God. First of all though, Paul reiterates that those Roman Gentiles were just sinners and unbelievers and plain ole pagans. But they had obtained salvation by obtaining mercy from God. Mercy was not getting what we all deserved by being miserable sinners, that is, hell and damnation. It is the Lord Jesus Christ, "by whom we have received grace..." (Romans 1:5), who has forgiven and saved us.

The Gentiles in Rome, just us Gentiles today, before they were saved, and bestowed

CHAPTER 4: ROMANS 11

mercy upon, did not believe God. But because of Israel's unbelief and rejection of the Messiah the Gentiles have received mercy to be open to the Gospel. The way was made open for salvation to the Gentiles because the Jews stumbled, and we need to always keep that in mind.

Even now, as the Jewish people as a whole do not believe in the Lord Jesus Christ as Messiah, that we should be merciful to Jews so that they can obtain mercy. We should love them enough to give them God's words. The Greek word for the first use of mercy in Verse 31 is "Eleos", which is a special usage of the word mercy. Whereas the other three meanings for the word mercy in Verses 30-32 is to have pity, and be compassionate, "Eleos" is different and special.

It is an action to be executed by the believer towards the Jew. It could even be considered a command from Christ Jesus. This mercy is not passive but more proactive. It is an immediate, sensitive regard to someone's misery which is the consequence of sins. It is a showing of the alleviation for such a consequence of sin is a result of the guilt and power of sin being removed by the cleansing power of the blood of Christ. It is the boldness in taking the Gospel to Jewish sinners that is the practiced mercy stated in this verse.

Verse 32 tells us that every person in this world is imprisoned or bottled up in unbelief and sin, but in this present time, the age of grace, has been offered the promise of Christ's mercy in the receiving of the Gospel. Everybody is affected by sin and the provision for forgiveness of sins is thereby offered to all. The Gospel is for all, Jew or Gentile.

Paul's Response to God's Ways Vs. 33-36

1. *the depth of the riches both of the wisdom and knowledge of God! How unsearchable are his judgments, and his ways past finding out!*
2. *For who hath known the mind of the Lord? Or who hath been his counsellor?*
3. *Or who hath first given to him, and it shall be recompensed unto him again?*
4. *For of him, and through him, and to him, are all things: To whom be glory forever. Amen.*

After writing Chapters 9-11, which involved his fellow lost kinsmen, which revealed God's plan for Israel, Paul launches into a laudatory, faith-filled strain of praise and adoration to God. This is Paul writing worship in words that express what man's limited mind can bring before the creator. It is man's difficulty understanding and reaching comprehension of the wisdom and ways of

CHAPTER 4: ROMANS 11

God. The words he uses about the depth of God's riches of wisdom and knowledge describe them as unsearchable. It is seeing a small part of what God is but it is impossible for man to see all.

Paul was honored that he was chosen to:

> *"Preach among the Gentiles the unsearchable riches of Christ."* (Ephesians 3:8b)

Paul prayed that all believers would be blessed by God.

> *"That Christ may dwell in your hearts...grounded in love, may be able to comprehend with all saints what is the breadth, and length, and depth, and height; and to know the love of Christ, which passeth knowledge,"* (Ephesians 3:17-19)

As men and women of God, it is beyond our limits to search out what God has done for man, why he has done so, and it is way past us to even find out. We can only praise him.

Verse 34 continues the thought that God is so above man, who can know all the mind of God?

> *"For he knoweth not that which shall be. For who can tell him when it shall be?"* (Eccl. 8:17)

God is in control and we are just his servants. God does control all that we can know because he made us to be able to mentally analyze beyond what he reveals to us.

No one can be God's counsellor or advise him what to do. No one can tell God, after he has designed what to do, how then to execute those plans. That is why Paul was so overwhelmed at how God operated through the history of man. He wanted to know how God performed all things, but had to give up at the magnificence of God and could only praise him.

In Verse 35 Paul makes it clear that since we are the created creature, there is no time that God will not come out as needing anything or can be supplemented in any way. It is God who rescues us by grace, preserving us by his mercy. We love him because he first loved us. We cannot do anything first for God that will add to God in any way. He is Alpha and Omega, the beginning the end.

> *"With whom took he counsel, and who instructed him, and taught him in the path of judgment, and taught him knowledge, and shewed to him the way of understanding?"* (Isaiah 40:14)

In Verse 36, Paul is so overwhelmed and so appreciative of God's salvation, he sums up all his accolades for God. It is because of God that we have salvation, for he has sent his son, Jesus Christ, to shed his blood to pay for our sins. It was because God opened the way to

CHAPTER 4: ROMANS 11

the Gentiles to come unto him and to put into place the plan to graft Israel back in, that he deserves praise and all the glory.

> *"And when all things shall be subdued unto him, then shall the Son also himself be subject unto him that put all things under him, that God may be all in all."* (1 Corinthians 15:28)

CHAPTER 5

Supersessionism and Antisemitism

Introduction

When looking at two very large subjects such as the two being of this present chapter, a narrow focus will be the extent of the investigation due to space constraints.

There are three interrelated concepts that are controlling the doctrine of Replacement Theology:

1. Belief in the interpretative priority of the NT over the OT.
2. Belief in nonliteral fulfillments of OT texts regarding Israel.
3. Belief that National Israel is a type of the NT church.[1]

George Ladd says that the New Testament (NT) interprets Old Testament (OT) prophecies differing from OT context, and that a literal interpretation of OT prophecies is not defensible. This leads to the thinking of the promises made to Israel are fulfilled in the Church. The restoration of Israel is brought into question by such a view. Their bottom line (of the supersessionists) is that the NT interprets, and/or re-interprets the Old Testament.

According to the second premise of the Replacement Theologists (R.T.'s), they hold the belief that the NT has nonliteral fulfillments of God's prophecies and promises to Israel. There are OT passages that clearly show future restoration to Israel (Amos 9:11-15; Zechariah 14:16; Joel 3:17-18) for example. Supersessionists get around this by arguing that said restoration has been fulfilled in other, nonliteral ways. They point to the three NT texts in particular proving their nonliteral fulfillments, (Acts 2:16-21; Acts 15:15-18; and Romans 9:24-26). Romans 9:24-26 will be looked at here.

The third belief supersessionists argue for is "typological interpretation." This is stated as being that the OT shows primarily types, shadows, and pictures of coming NT things. They use typological interpretation, which is different than a belief in OT types, to understand the Bible. We cannot ignore types in the OT and we cannot treat everything in the OT as types, pictures, and shadows as the supersessionists do.

Definition

The word supersessionism comes from the English verb "to supersede," from the Latin verb "sedere," to sit, plus "super" upon. It

CHAPTER 5: SUPERSESSIONISM AND ANTISEMITISM

thus signifies one thing being replaced or supplanted by another.[2]

Supersessionism is also called replacement theology or fulfillment theology. Three types of supersessionism are held by replacement theologians.

The first is punitive supersessionism which says that because the Jewish nation has rejected the Messiah, God has punished Israel by displacing them as his people. "Because the Jews obstinately reject God's action in Christ, God in turn angrily rejects and punishes the Jews."[3]

This view was held by Hippolytus, Origen, and Martin Luther. Luther felt that the destruction of Jerusalem, the scattering of the Jews, and the destruction of the Temple and their priesthood, were all proofs of God's permanent rejection of them.

The second type of supersessionism is "economic" supersessionism. This says that it was God's plan to have an expiration date as being God's people and that their role was to be passed onto another entity that was universal and non-ethnic in character. Yes, Israel was disobedient, but with the coming of Jesus Christ now is replaced by a new spiritual Israel, the Church.

The danger of economic supersessionism, is that, since punitive supersessionism may be rejected with ease by Christians, its premise of an obsolete Israel may linger. Christians could be lured into thinking that Israel's existence is expired in God's eyes but that God will still be faithful to her even in unbelief. Writers in support of economic supersessionism include Justin Martyr, Augustine, and Karl Barth.

There is a third type of supersessionism, identified by Soulen, as being structural supersessionism. This mainly concerns the Jewish scriptures,

> "whereby it renders the Hebrew scriptures large indecisive for shaping Christian convictions about how God works as consummator and a redeemer engage humankind in universal and enduring ways."[4]

The result of this approach is the removal of the Hebrew Scriptures from having a voice. This plays into their view of having the NT scriptures superseding the original meanings of OT passages.

Replacement

Replacement theology, declared that the Church, Abraham's spiritual seed, had replaced National Israel in that it had transcended and fulfilled the terms of the covenant given to Israel, which covenant Israel had lost because of disobedience.[5]

CHAPTER 5: SUPERSESSIONISM AND ANTISEMITISM

The Roman Catholic Church teaches supersessionism but will not call it that. They teach the fulfillment of the Mosaic Covenant and its replacement in the New Covenant, which makes the Catholic Church the "new Israel." The Jews to them are only symbolic of the gifts and blessings of God are still available. However, they are also in unbelief of the Gospel and have not obtained mercy.

The views of the Protestants stem from their understanding of the covenants of the Bible, particularly the relationship between the Covenants of the Old Testament and the New Covenant. The main groups concerned with this relationship are Covenant Theology, New Covenant Theology and Dispensationalism.

Did God abandon Israel and replace Israel with the Christian church with all the promises, prophesies, and covenants? Supersessionism in our time has been pointed out for its mistreatment of the Jews in the past. It is a doctrinal (false) teaching that began from the very early church with Justin Martyr being the first to identify the Church as Israel.[6]

Between the period of 100 A.D. and 430 A.D. the idea grew among Christian leaders to blame the Jews, calling them Christ killers. These Patristic Era fathers blamed Christ's crucifixion on the Jewish people as a whole. Added to this early stage of Christian Anti-

Semitism was the insistence of the predominantly Gentile Church that God had abandoned the Jews and that the Church was now the true Israel. Thus, from the Anti-Semitic roots of the early Church was supersessionism born.

Positions of Supersessionists

When it comes to Israel there are two main groups of Christians: those who are pro-Israel are called "Christian Zionists" and those who are supersessionists and believe Israel has no place in prophecy. It is said that the latter group is in the majority and hold to one or more of the following:

1. Covenant theology
2. Amillennialism- which says there is no literal 1000 year reign of Christ on Earth.
3. Preterism – which says all the promises of God and blessings occurred in 70 A.D. and all was transferred to the church as a replacement.
4. They say Book of Revelation written before 70 A.D.
5. OT references of blessing for the children of Israel refer to the "people of God" not the nation of Israel.
6. Terms like "the Great Tribulation," Armageddon," and Rapture of the church" not treated as literal events of future prophetic fulfillment.

CHAPTER 5: SUPERSESSIONISM AND ANTISEMITISM

7. Allegorical interpretation of Bible Prophecy rather than literal and historical.[7]

Premises

1. Israel, the Jewish people and the land, has been replaced by the Christian Church. The Church is the historic continuation of Israel to the exclusion of the former.
2. The Jewish people are now no longer a "chosen people".
3. Apart from repenting and being born-again, and being part of the Church, the Jews have no future, no hope, and no calling in the plan of God.
4. Since Pentecost in Acts 2, the term "Israel" refers only to the Church.
5. The promises, blessings, and covenants once given to the Jews have been taken away and given to the Church. The Jews are still subject to the curses found in the Bible, as a result of their rejection of Christ.[8]

The Jews are a separate people to whom pertains the adoption, the glory, the covenants, the promises, the law, and the service of God (Romans 9:4)

God has not revoked the gifts and calling to his people. (Romans 11:29). There are numerous places in the New Testament that only refer to Israel and not the Church. Paul in talking to believers in Romans 10:1, and prays that Israel might be saved, for it does not pertain to the Church to be saved who already were, for example. The promises made to Abraham in Genesis 12:1-3 are everlasting promises made to Israel. There are promises God has made to Israel and the Jewish people and God's affirmation of these is found in Jeramiah 31: 35-37. God's promises to a future Israel will be fulfilled according to Romans 11: 25-27.

> "The error of Replacement Theology is like a cancer in the Church that headache not only caused it to violate God's word concerning the Jewish people and Israel, but it made us into instruments of hate, not love, in God's name. Yet, it is not too late to change our ways and rightly relate to the Jewish people and Israel today."[9]

The errors of the supersessionists have led them to preach:

> "If Christians will quit supporting Israel and will economically boycott the Christ-rejecting Jews, they will accept Jesus Christ."[10]

No boycott will result in a mass conversion of the Jews. It would only hurt them and cause unnecessary misery. The crusades attempted economic destruction of the Jews. They took everything and the Jews did not convert. The Inquisition made the Roman

CHAPTER 5: SUPERSESSIONISM AND ANTISEMITISM

Catholic Church rich from Jewish wealth and that did not result in a mass conversion. The Nazi's tried and achieved some horrible success but in the end failed. They took away their jobs, destroyed their businesses in the infamous Kristallnacht, and then fined them to pay for repairs that the Nazi henchmen inflicted(Shades of Baltimore today in some respects). Even after six million Jews were killed in gas chambers, they did not become Christians. God has already planned for Israel's future, supersessionists need not worry.

1. All Israel will be saved (Romans 11:26)
2. Israel will look on the Messiah and accept him (Zechariah 12:10)
3. Israel will be forgiven of all sin (Romans 11:27)

Non-Literal Fulfillment?

Returning to Replacement arguments for nonliteral fulfillments of Old Testament promises of prophecy, promises, and covenants, certain Scriptures are used to hold to such false doctrines. Several casual, non-study readings of the Bible, lean toward a future restoration of Israel. In Amos 9, God shares the truth that Israel will be restored by Him to the land. Zechariah 14 and Joel 3 tell of worship of the Lord in a future Jerusalem and future prosperity of Israel respectively.

Three main texts are cited by supersessionists as being important to their argument. They are: Acts 2:16-21; 15:15-18; and Romans 9:24-26.

The first, Acts 2:16-21, in which Peter quotes Joel 2:28-31. Israel's future restoration is indicated as well as a fulfillment that happened at Pentecost. Joel 2:28 says in part, "I will pour out my spirit upon all flesh; and your sons and daughters shall prophecy." This did happen on Pentecost as Peter spoke, and the rest of the prophecy refers to the coming of the day of the Lord, which will be terrible. To supersessionists this is just a continuation of Israel in the Church as it is reconstituted.

Another part of Scripture mishandled by supersessionists is Romans 9:24-26. Clearly, Paul in quoting Hosea, is confirming that God is going to go to the Gentiles to call out a people for Himself. He was going to call any Jews who would hear, but also the call was to go out to the Gentiles. To a people who were not God's people (the Gentiles) were going to be the sons of God, since the Apostasy of Israel had put such a bad stink in God's nostrils. However, the supersessionists refuse rightly dividing of the words of God. They mistake the future prophesies meant for Israel to be fulfilled in the Church, which God was just forming. Since God was calling both Jews

CHAPTER 5: SUPERSESSIONISM AND ANTISEMITISM

and Gentiles, they were supposed to be the new people of God in the new Israel. Therefore, the prophesies of Hosea are to be fulfilled in the Christian Church.[12]

Richardson says that the prophesy in Hosea means:

> "God has raised up a new Israel and made with her a new covenant, because the old Israel had failed to keep the promise."[13]

Romans 11:26

Romans 9-11 has been shown earlier to be a detailed treatment of Israel not to be found elsewhere in the NT. The central question asked by Paul which is still sparking debate is:

> "I say then, hath God cast away his people?" (Romans 11:1)

It's a question whose answer has tripped up the supersessionists ever since, "God forbid." Never mind that Paul in Verse 2 explained the mystery of the total blindness of part of Israel, and that this blindness was a result of Israel's rejection of Jesus Christ as the Messiah. The time element was also included; "until the fullness of the Gentiles be come in." It must still be a mystery to some who should be enlightened by now. It is not the completed church, but when the last Gentile kingdom will be destroyed by the Lord Jesus Christ. That last kingdom will be Anti-

Christ's and it will not be able to stand because without the faith of believers of the Lord Jesus Christ be present, then there is no basis for the Gentile power or authority.

So, when Jesus Christ shall destroy the Anti-Christ system, then, "all Israel shall be saved." This is based on Zechariah 13:8-9. The deliverer shall come, the third be left therein, and their sins shall be forgiven. The correct meaning of all Israel will be the third of the population of Jews that have been preserved by Christ through the Tribulation, around three million. The timing of Israel's salvation is the setting up of the Millennial Kingdom by our Lord Jesus Christ.

Supersessionists have a very difficult time with the interpretation of "all Israel." That's understandable. They believe:

1. All Israel includes believer Jews and Gentiles, a group they call the elect. To them it is happening now. Christ is saving Jews and Gentiles and they, right now, make up the true Israel - The Church.

Robertson thinks he knows what Paul meant to say:

> "and in this manner (kai houtos), by such a fantastic process which shall throughout the present age 'up to' (archrishon) the point where the full

CHAPTER 5: SUPERSESSIONISM AND ANTISEMITISM

number of the Gentiles is brought in, all Israel is saved."[14]

The Church is composed of both Jew and Gentile, and it is within the Church that there is neither Jew, Gentile, male or female.

> *"For there is no difference between the Jew and the Greek:"* (Romans 10:12a)

The Church will be gone before the beginning of the Tribulation and return with Christ when he sets up His Kingdom.

> *"And the armies which were in Heaven followed him upon white horses, clothed in fine linen, white and clean."* (Revelation 19:14)

The other two interpretations; that "all Israel" includes the total number of elect Jews throughout history; and that there will be a mass conversion of Jews into the Church, are conjecture and myth and no scripture supports them.

This is a brief look at a terrible disgrace that started long ago in the early church with Justin Martyr. This false doctrine of supersessionism on the replacement of Israel with the Church is diabolical and has gripped the entirety of the Church to the point that more than a majority support their claims. Whether supersessionists have made their case or not, the damage inflicted upon low-information Christians is evidence of this present evil. Christians need to be taught, and learn on their own the Biblical revelation that God has given us concerning latter times Israel and its restoration.

But this is only one head of the two-headed monster.

Antisemitism

Whereas, supersessionism is an early church-born false doctrine, it is hideous for its infection throughout the Church up to and including our present time. It is one of the ugly heads of the two-headed snake. Antisemitism is the second head, and though it can be argued that its beginnings were in the church, it has poured out and overspread the whole earth like a cancer.

The early Church aided Jewish mistreatment which reached an inhuman character with the coming of Constantine with his establishment of his Christian empire in the fourth century. He started to transform anti-Semitic doctrine into anti-Semitic law. This was all a result of Replacement theology and all of its degradations being very detrimental to the Jews. Starting in 315 A.D. up to the Council of Basel in 1434 A.D., the Jew was removed from Christian society and locked them behind Ghetto walls.[15]

CHAPTER 5: SUPERSESSIONISM AND ANTISEMITISM

It was at the Synod of Breslau in 1267 that Jews were in fact forced to reside in ghettos.[16]

The result of centuries of anti-Semitic laws was predictable. There has been a long, long history of anti-Jewish violence, which includes charges of deicide, blood libels, the Crusades, the Inquisitions, countless pogroms and other massacres. It needs to be noted that Constantine's rule evolved into the Roman Catholic Church that carried on the violence in the name of Christ. Anti-Semitic edicts and anti-Semitic acts continued in Protestant areas as much as it did in Rome's sphere of influence.

What is Anti-Semitism?

This term is first found in Der Sieg des Judenthums uber das Germanenthum ("The Victory of Judaism over Germanism") by Wilhelm Marr (1879).[17]

Very simply, Anti-Semitism is hatred for the Jews.

The U.S. State Department on their website has a working definition of Anti-Semitism.

> "Anti-Semitism is a certain perception of Jews, which may be expressed as hatred toward Jews. Rhetorical and physical manifestations of Anti-Semitism are directed toward Jewish or non-Jewish individuals and/or their property, toward

Jewish community institutions and religious facilities."[18]

The EUMC explains that certain acts could include the targeting of the State of Israel. They write that Anti-Semitism is a mask from which it charges Jews with conspiracy to harm humanity, and to always blame Jews for "why things go wrong." Methods employed include writings, speeches, visual forms and actions, using dark stereotypes and bad character traits. A big worldwide contemporary example of this would be the Holocaust denial movement. This would include accusing the Jews as a people, or Israel as a state of inventing or exaggerating the Holocaust. Another sinister example of current antisemitism would be the use of symbols and images associated with classic Anti-Semitism such as the Jews killed Jesus or blood libel.

In the case of blood libel, it has started since the Middle Ages, around the 1100s. Jews were accused of killing Gentile or Christian children for ritualistic purposes. It was said that they drained the blood from their victims to be an ingredient in the Passover Matzo. In the past, anti-Jewish riots and mass-murders followed such allegations. The truth is that kosher dietary laws that were written by God in Exodus and Leviticus forbid the use of blood and that blood must be drained from all meats before they are eaten.

CHAPTER 5: SUPERSESSIONISM AND ANTISEMITISM

There has not been any proof of any killing of Christian children by any Jew for over 900 years.

For some reason, in recent years, Texe Marrs claimed that Jews were killing Christian children to use their blood for the feast of Purim cookies! Marrs makes up a story as fact about the book of Esther. He states that Esther, who was very beautiful, seduced King Ahasuerus and then tricked him into saving the Jewish people. Her uncle, Mordecai, was a conniver who helped Esther, and that Haman was the good guy who was framed and then murdered by Esther and Mordecai.

Attitudes

We, as Christians are commanded by God to take the Gospel to the Jewish people so that they may be saved. By the Christian's obedience to God's will for his life and joy in the Lord is to provoke them to jealousy (Romans 11:11) so that they will want to receive Christ as Savior. The Devil wants to upset God's will and provoke the Jewish people to fear and anger, because he wants the Jews to suffer God's eternal wrath. The Devil plants unscriptural attitudes in the hearts and minds to accomplish his will.

  2. The only good Jew is a dead or converted (to Catholicism) Jew. (Popular slogan during Inquisition.

3. When a Jew receives Jesus as Lord and Savior he or she stops being a Jew.
4. God is through with the Jewish people because they had their chance and blew it.
5. The Jewish people have suffered over these past two thousand years because they crucified Jesus.
6. Jews who believe in Jesus should be segregated from Gentile Christians and not be part of the Church.
7. The Great Commission to carry the Gospel to the uttermost part of the earth does not include sharing with Jewish neighbors and friends in the next office or down the block. Why not? Because Jews no longer matter to God.
8. The Jewish people suffered enough in the Holocaust, and the Church should just leave them alone.
9. The Jewish people have their own Sinaitic Covenant with God and need to live in accordance with the Law of Moses.
10. A person born Jewish should remain Jewish and not seek to become a Christian.[19]

Satan's imprint is all over these nine attitudes. These attitudes can only hurt relations between Jewish people who need the Gospel and Christians.

CHAPTER 5: SUPERSESSIONISM AND ANTISEMITISM

Martin Luther

Some words need to be said about Martin Luther and his relation to Jews and Judaism. Luther went through two separate periods of two different attitudes towards Jews. The first period he was sympathetic and compassionate for their misery and wanted them to get saved. The first pamphlet he wrote concerning the Jews was "Dass Jesus ein Geborner Jud Sei." In 1543. In it he accuses the Roman Catholic Church was so repulsive in its form of Christianity that no Jew could ever be won over to Jesus. He is quoted as saying,

> "I would advise and beg everybody to deal kindly with the Jews, instruct them in the Scriptures, we could expect them to come over to us."

Then just one year later in 1544, Luther penned two books which are filled with bitterness towards the Jews. "Von den Juden und Ihren Leugen" (Concerning the Jews and Their Lies); and Vom Schem Hamphoras und Vom Geschlecht Christi" (of the unknowable name and the Generations of Christ). The latter book describes as being equal with the Devil and used vile language about them. "Schem Hamphoras" is the Hebrew sacred name of God, the Tetragrammaton. The use of the four letter, JHWA, or Jehovah God was an insult to Jewish sensitivities.

In that book he describes a carving in a parish church depicting a sow under which young pigs and Jews are sucking. There is a rabbi behind a leg of the sow looking intently into the Talmud, as if he is reading. He writes that it is here they received their Shem Hamphoras.

This sort of vulgarity with a vengeance appealed to the Germans in his region. Luther wanted the German Jews to enter Christianity and join forces with him to go after all the scandal, false teachings, and corruption in the Roman Catholic Church. The Jews chose to remain Jews and so Luther unleashed his venom on them, the Jews. He became deeply Anti-Semitic and claimed the Jews were no longer God's chosen people but "the Devil's people."[20]

It turns out that Luther's Anti-Semitism in Germany deeply appealed to Adolph Hitler. The Nazis used Luther's texts to build up their Anti-Semitism and incorporated them into the school's curriculum. They also promoted Luther into the sermons in Lutheran Churches.[21]

> "What Hitler did was only putting Luther's war plans into reality. Indeed, everything Hitler did to the Jews...had already been done...before by the Christian churches, especially the Catholic Church. Hitler learned it all from the

CHAPTER 5: SUPERSESSIONISM AND ANTISEMITISM

Catholic Church.[22]

The following is taken from "The War" page 116, and sums up what Martin Luther is remembered for:

> "This terrible man was a predecessor of Hitler. He demanded that all Jews not only become slaves, as Saint Augustine ordained, but he made slaves of the serfs, so he might never touch the hand of a Christian German."

In his tract "Shem Hamphoresh" (1544) Luther referred to the Jews as ritual murderers, poisoners of wells and, since they were worse than devils, demanded the burning of 'all their synagogues and Talmuds.'

Here is what the foremost Protestant leader recommends for the Jews:

> 'they should be forced to hardest labor as handymen or serfs only; they should not be permitted to hold services; every Christian should be admonished to deal with them in a merciless manner; if you suffer, strike them in the jaw; if I had the power, I would assemble them to prove to us that we Christians do not worship God, under penalty of having their tongues cut out through the back of their necks.'

Luther's references to the Jews in his pamphlet "Die Juden und irhe Lugen (About the Jews and their Lies) are not repeatable. They are course, vile, vicious, and vulgar."

The Protocols

There is one tool of anti-Jewish propaganda that stands alone in its influence for the atrocities against Jews for the entire 20th Century up to this day. It is the "Protocols of the Learned Elders of Zion."

Protocols are original drafts, minutes, or a record of a document or transaction. The "Protocols" were one of many pamphlets circulated before the first World War.

> "Pamphlet prepared and distributed by the Czarist government after Russia's defeat at the hands of the Japanese (1905). The Jew was to be the scapegoat for a corrupt and discredited government.
>
> In 1921 a correspondent of the London Times uncovered the plagiarism of half the "Protocols" from a satire on Napoleon III written by Maurice Joly, a French attorney. Other portions were plagiarized from a story by Hermann Goedsche and other fictional sources." [23]
>
> "Jewish conspiracy theories have been traced back to the New Testament's imputation of responsibility to the Sanhedrin for calling for the arrest of Jesus and abounded in the Medieval World. In its standard modern formulation, the Jews or Zionists form a powerful, secret, global cabal that manipulates governmental institutions, banks, the media, and other institutions for malevolent purposes,

CHAPTER 5: SUPERSESSIONISM AND ANTISEMITISM

> undermining decent purposes. "The Protocols of the Elders of Zion, a fraudulent document purporting to record a Jewish plan for world domination, has influenced countless ideas about supposed Jewish global conspiracies including, notably, ideas contained within the Hamas Charter. This may also be seen in accusations that Israel or the Jewish people are responsible for virtually any contemporary catastrophe, such as the attack on the World Trade Center on September 11, 2001." [24]

The "Protocols" were published in several editions helped by religious writer and mystic, Serge Nilus. With each new printed edition came a new story about how he obtained the document. On one such edition he claimed to have stolen the document from a non-existent Zionist headquarters in France.

> "The Protocols were actually written in Paris sometime between 1895 and 1899 by an agent of the Russian Secret Police, Mathieu Golovinski, who copied most of it from a French satire on Napoleon III that had nothing to do with Jewish people. The forgery was an attempt to destroy the Bolshevik-led political movement to modernize Russia by linking it to a Jewish plot to destroy Western Civilization."[25]

Its Influence

The Russian Revolution that led that country to become Communist, was led by the Bolsheviks in 1917. The supporters of the overthrown Czar charged the Bolsheviks as being a willing part of a Jewish plot to enslave the world. The "Protocols" were pointed to as the blueprint being followed, and spread with even more viciousness by Soviet dictator Joseph Stalin.

The idea of a Jewish Conspiracy moved to Britain in the 1920s. It was there that two British reporters published the "Protocols" in the "Morning Post." The following accompanied the article:

> "The Jews are carrying out with steadfast purpose, creating wars and revolutions...to destroy the white Gentile race, that the Jews may seize power during the resulting chaos and rule with their claimed superior intelligence over the remaining races of the word, as kings over slaves."[26]

The "Protocols" were published in the U.S. by Boris Brasol who had been a lawyer in Czarist Russia.[27]

After that Henry Ford was responsible for popularizing the "Protocols" through the United States. Ford had occult ties and believed in reincarnation. He had a close friendship with Thomas Alva Edison, who was a faithful theosophist, who are into the occult and New Age beliefs.

> "Theosophy, its doctrine, its foundress, and its adherents, can all be

CHAPTER 5: SUPERSESSIONISM AND ANTISEMITISM

shown to have been involved in racism, conspiracy, theories, and at least one Anti-Semitic tract."[28]

Ford had published many articles on the "Protocols" in one of his newspapers, the "Dearborn Independent." These were later published in a book, "The International Jew: The World's Foremost Problem." Because of this, and wide circulation, hundreds of thousands of people worldwide were exposed to the "Protocols" as the truth.

The "Protocols" were in Germany around the year 1918, brought to it by Alfred Rosenberg. Hitler got a hold of them by the early 1920's and it formed the basis for "Mein Kampf. The myth of Jewish world domination was the driving force behind the Nazis push to eradicate the Jews. They passed Anti-Semitic laws, unleased "Kristallnacht," and ending the "Final Solution."

The "Protocols" have become a major source of Arab and Islamic propaganda today. An example is what appears in the Hamas Charter:

> "The Zionist plan is limitless. After Palestine, the Zionists aspire to expand from the Nile to the Euphrates. When they have digested the region they overtook, they will aspire to further expansion, and so on. Their plan is embodied in the Protocols of the Elders of Zion, and their present

conduct is the best proof of what we are sayng."²⁹

We thus see the character of the people and of the "Protocols" themselves and the fanatical hatred (Anti-Semitism) for the Jews. Christians must adhere to the Scriptures condemning such Anti-Semitism which Paul summed up.

> *"Boast not against the branches...that blindness in part is happened to Israel, until the fullness of the Gentiles be come in, but as touching the election, they are beloved for the fathers' sakes." (Romans 11:18a, 25b, 28b)*

ENDNOTES

Introduction

1. Dagabert D. Runes. *The War Against the Jew.* Preface. p 1x.
2. *The Hamas Charter.* Stand With Us. Los Angeles. 2014.
3. Ibid.
4. Ibid
5. Ken Spiro. *The Miracle of Jewish History.* 1995.
6. Lundberg. *The Jew and Modern Israel.* p 90.
7. Spiro. *Miracle.* 1995.
8. Ibid.
9. Ken L. Markus. *Elements of Anti-Semitism.* Brandeis Ctr. 2010.
10. The Atlantic. *The World is Full of Holocaust Deniers.* 2014.
11. Wikipedia. *Holocaust Denial.* 2014.
12. *Negationism in General.* Chap. 1. 2002.
13. *Austin App.* Wikipedia. 2014.
14. Stephen Atkins. *Austin J. App and Holocaust Denial.* Westport, CT. 2009. pp 153-155.
15. *Willis A. Carto: Fabricating History.* Anti-Defamation League. 2001.
16. Deborah Lipstadt. *Denying the Holocaust.* Free Press. New York. 1993. p 77.
17. *Elmer Barnes.* Wikipedia.
18. *Negationism in General.* Voiceofdharma.com.
19. Ibid.
20. Ibid.
21. Spoken during conference marking 40th anniversary of the Legal Services Corporation.

22. Abraham Foxman. *Chides Joe Biden for using term, Shylock*. CNN.com. 09/07/2014.
23. Phillipe Burrin. *Nazi Anti-Semitism: From Prejudice to Holocaust*. the New Pres. 2005.
24. Bob Glaze. Email to Charles Kriessman. *Israel*. 12/13/2014

CHAPTER 1

1. Adam Clarke. *Commentary*. Vol. 1 p 139.
2. Ibid. p 160.
3. Ibid. p 168.
4. Ibid. p 183.
5. Theodore Robinson. *A History of Israel*. Vol. I. p 62.
6. Adam Clarke. *Commentary*. Volume I. p 235.
7. Ibid. p 269.
8. Ibid. p 119.
9. Ibid. p 325.
10. Ibid. p 357.
11. Ibid. p 307.
12. Ibid. p 350.
13. Mason. *Prophetic Problems*. Moody Press. p 29.
14. Ibid. p 32.
15. Ibid. p 35.
16. Fruchtenbaum. *The Eight Covenants of the Bible*.
17. Cruden. *Cruden's Complete Concordance*. 1968. p 725.
18. Ibid. Part II. p 18.
19. Ibid. Part II. p 18.
20. Cloud. *Believer's Bible Dictionary*. p 28.
21. McIntosh. *Notes on Exodus*. 1862. p 267.
22. Moorman. *Conies, Brass, and Easter*. Culled from information on Brass.
23. Soltau. *The Holy Vessels*. p 111.

24. B.F.T. *Defined King James Bible*. Footnote. p 113.
25. Dettaan. *The Tabernacle*. p 105.

CHAPTER 2

1. Schweitzer. *A History of Jews Since the First Century*. A.D. 1971. New York. p 35.
2. Sarles. *angelolgy*. pp 4-5.
3. Waite. *Romans*. p 352.
4. Ibid. p 384.

CHAPTER 3

1. Waite. *Romans*. p 411.

CHAPTER 4

1. Kreloff. *Gods Plan for Israel*. p 81.
2. Carmel. *Jesus in the Seven Feasts*. p 41.
3. Stifler. *Epistle to the Romans*. p 193.

CHAPTER 5

1. Vlach. *Has Church Replaced Israel?* p 79.
2. Wikipedia. *Supersessionism*.
3. Soulen. *The God of Israel*. p 30.
4. Ibid. p 181.
5. W.C. Kairser. *An Assessment of replacement Theology*. p 9.
6. Justin Martyr. *Dialogue with Trypho*. p 11.
7. David Hocking. *Attack of Replacement Theology*. p 1.
8. Clarence Wagner. *The Error of Replacement Theology*. p 1.
9. Clarence Wagner. *Bridges for Peace*. Speech. 2003.
10. Earl Paulk. *To Whom is God Betrothed?* p 40.
11. Hagee. *In Defense of Israel*. p 148.
12. Ladd. *Historic Premillennialism*. p 24.

13. A. Richardson. *An Introduction to the Theology of the New Testament.* p 270.
14. Robertson. *The Israel of God.* 167-192. From Vlach. p 138.
15. Brog. *Standing with Israel.* pp 26-27.
16. Ibid. p 27.
17. The European Monitoring Center on Racism and Xenophobia.
18. Dagobert Runes. *The War.* p 6.
19. Telchin. *Abandoned.* pp 35-36.
20. Luther. *Vom Schem Hamphoras.* Quoted in Michael. 113
21. *Luther Quarterly.* Spring 1987
22. Runes. *The War.* p xvii
23. Ibid. pp 150-151
24. Brandeis Center. *Fact Sheet of Anti-Semitic Discourse.* p 3.
25. Anti-Defamation League. *A Hoax of Hate.* 2010.
26. Ibid. p 2.
27. Ibid. p 2.
28. Cumbey. *A Planned Deception.* p 96.
29. Anti-Defamation League. *A Hoax of Hate.* p 3.

BIBLIOGRAPHY

Books

Allensworth, Norman W. *Witnessing To the Jewish People.* L.A. Messiamic Witness. Van Nuys, CA. 1960.

Arendt, Hannah. *Antisemitism.* Harcourt Brace Jovanovich Publishers. Orlando, FL. 1985.

Brog, David. *Standing with Israel.* Frontline. Lake Mary, Florida. 2006.

Brown, Michael L. *Our Hands Are Stained With Blood.* ICN Ministries. Pensacola, FL. 1997.

Carmel, Douglas. *Jesus in the Seven Feasts of Israel.* Rock of Israel Ministries. Fairfield, OH. 2013.

Carroll, James. *Constantine's Sword.* First Mariner Books. 2002.

Cloud, David W. *Believer's Bible Dictionary.* Way of Life Literature. Port Huron, MI. 2015.

Cumbey, Constance E. *A Planned Deception.* Pointe Publishers, Inc. East Detroit, Michigan. 1985. pp. 90-100.

DeHaan, M.R. *The Tabernacle.* Zondervan Publishing. Grand Rapids, MI. 1983.

Eckardt, Alice and Roy. *Encounter With Israel.* Association Press. New York. 1970.

Erdman, Charles R. *Epistle of Paul to the Romans.* Westminster Press. Philadelphia, PA 1966.

Estep, Howard C. *Petra.* World Prophetic Ministry, Inc. Colton, CA. 1970.

Flannery, Edward H. *The Anguish of the Jews.* The Macmillan Company. New York. 1965.

Goldstein, Phyllis. *A Convenient Hatred: The History of Antisemitism.* Facing History and Ourselves. Brookline, MA. 2012.

Hagee, John. *In Defense of Israel.* Frontline. Lake Mary, Florida. 2007.

Hay, Malcolm. *The Roots of Christian Anti-Semitism.* Freedom Library Press. New York. 1981.

Hodge, Charles. *The Epistle to the Romans.* The Banner of Truth Trust. Chatham. Great Britain. 1989.

Hull, William L. *The Fall and Rise of Israel.* Zondervan Publishing House. Grand Rapids, Michigan. 1978.

Hutchings, N.W. *Romance of Romans.* Hearthstone Publishing. Oklahoma City, OK. 1990. pp 300-376.

Isaac, Jules. *Has Anti-Semitism Roots in Christianity?* National Conference of Christians and Jews. New York.

Kreloff, Steven A. *God's Plan for Israel.* Loizeaux Publishing. 1995.

Laqueur, Walter. *A History of Zionism.* MJF Books. New York.

_____ *The Changing Face of Anti-Semitism."* Oxford University Press. New York. 2006.

Lipstadt, Deborah. *Denying the Holocaust.* The Free Press. A Division of Macmillan, Inc. New York. 1993.

Littell, Franklin H. *The Crucifixion of the Jews.* Harper and Row Publishers. 1975.

McIntosh, C.H. *Notes on the Book of Exodus.* George Morrish. London. 3rd Edition. 1862.

McQuaid, Elwood. *The Zion Connection.* The Friends of Israel Gospel Ministry, Inc. Bellmawr, NJ. 2003.

ENDNOTES

McTernan, John + Koenig. *Israel the Blessing or the Curse.* Hearthstone Publishing. Oklahoma City, OK. 2002.

Moorman, Dr. J.A. *Conies, Brass, and Easter.* B.F.T. 31737. Collingswood, NJ.

Robinson, Theodore H. *A History of Israel.* Vol. I. Oxford University Press. 1951.

Runes, Dagobert D. *The War Against the Jew.* Philosophical Library, Inc.

Schaff, Thomas. *Romans.* Family Stations, Inc. Oakland, CA. Feb. 1999.

Simeon, Charles. *Expository Outlines on the Whole Bible.* Vol. 15 Romans. Zondervan. Grand Rapids, Michigan. 1955.

Soltau, Henry W. *The Tabernacle, The Priesthood and the Offerings.* Kregal Publications, Grand Rapids, MI. 1972.

_____. *The Holy Vessel and Furniture of the Tabernacle.* Kregal Publications. Grand Rapids, MI. 1971.

Soulen, Kendall R. *The God of Israel and Christian Theology.* Fortress Press. Minneapolis. 1996.

Spargimino, Dr. Larry. *The Anti-Prophets – The Challenge of Preterism.* Hearthstone Publishing. Oklahoma City, OK. 2000.

Stifler, James M. *Epistle to the Romans.* Moody Pres. Chicago. 1960.

Thomas, W.H. Griffith. *The Pentateuch.* Kregal Publication. Grand Rapid, MI. 1985.

_____. *St. Paul's Epistle to the Romans.* Eerdman's Publishing Co. Grand Rapids, MI 1970.

Vlach, Michael J. *Has the Church Replaced Israel?* B+H Academic Publishing. Nashville, TN 2010.

Waite, Dr. D.A. *Romans.* Bible For Today Press. Collingswood, NJ Oct. 2005. pp 351-456.

ARTICLES

Anti-Defamation League. *The Protocols of Zion.* 2010.

Bible-Study Tools. *Romans 9-11.* www.biblestudytools.com.

Bynum, E.L. *John Hagee.* Plains Baptist Challenger. May 2006.

Copeland, Mark A. *The Epistle to the Romans.* www.executableoutlines.com. 2011. Chapters 9-11.

Cowles, Mark. *Premillennialism: The Friend of Israel.* Foundation Magazine. Issue 4. 2008.

Fruchtenbaum, Dr. Arnold G. *The Eight Covenants of the Bible.* Messiamicassociation.org. Accessed 4/20/2015.

Hocking, David. *The Attacks of Replacement Theology.* Destiny Newsletter. March 2006.

In the Doghouse. *Ten Egyptian Plagues.* Inthedoghouse.hubpages.com. Accessed 03/18/2005.

Jewish Encyclopedia. *Luther, Martin.* Jewishencyclopedia.com 2002.

Karen, Herbert. "*The History of Israel's Blindness.*" Bibliotheca Sacra. Oct. 1937.

Kiesler, Herbert. "*Exegesis of Galatians 3:26-28.*" Bibliotheca Sacra. 1987.

Killough, Ashley. "*Biden says use of term 'Shylocks' was a poor choice.*" CNN.com Sept 2014.

Leverett, Bert. "*The Elijah Complex.*" Sermons.Logos.com. Accessed Article 5/18/15.

ENDNOTES

Rockwood, Perry F. *Studies in Galatians.* Peoples Gospel Hour. Nova Scotia, Canada.

Spurgeon. *Christ the End of the Law.* Spurgeon.org./sermons/1325. htm. Accessed 5/5/2015.

Tabb, Dr. M.H. *The Just Shall Live By Faith.* Foundation Ministries, FL. 1983 pp.87-107.

Wagner, Clarence H. *Christian Anti-Semitism.* Theirfinersfire.org. 1992.

_____. *The Error of Replacement Theology.* www.Idolphin.org/replacement.

Waite, Dr. D.A. *Christ Our Passover.* B.F.T. #129. 2001.

Wikipedia. *Holocaust Denial.* en.wikipedia.org. Accessed 12/30/2014.

_____. *Supersessionism.* en.wikipedia.org.

Williams, Dr. H.D. *Israel's Covenants.* A Conservative Bible Study, Lesson 5. Undated. Accessed theoldpaths.org. 2015.

_____. *Pentecost's Factors Concerning Israel's Blindness.* Theoldpaths.org. 2015. pp 1-8.

Yosef, Uri. *The Anti-Jewish New Testament.* Messiah Truth Project, Inc. 2001.

NOTE: This represents a small portion of nearly 100 articles consulted on the subject.

INDEX OF WORDS AND PHRASES

70 A.D., 12, 55, 165, 166, 167, 236, 254
Aaron, 79, 91, 152, 161, 162, 195
Abib, 106
Abrahamic Covenant, 9, 12, 69, 72, 117, 119, 123
Acacia wood, 159
Adam and Eve, 68
Adamic, 123
Africans, 32
Allegorical interpretation, 255
Al-Qaeda, 52
Anathema, 174
Anti-Defamation League, 31, 32, 275, 278, 282
Antisemitism, 10, 249, 262, 279, 280
Anti-Semitism, 3, 30, 31, 33, 37, 38, 43, 44, 47, 49, 55, 254, 263, 264, 268, 274, 275, 276, 280, 283
Arabs, 24, 44, 46, 53, 178
Assyrians, 30
Atonement, 142, 162
Auschwitz, 31, 38, 41
Austin App, 34, 36, 275
Baal, 170, 212, 213, 214
Babylon, 22, 165
Bar Kokhba, 167
Barnes Review, 37, 39
Billy Graham, 62
Blaise Pascal, 29
Blood, 113, 279
Boils, 101
Bolshevik, 46, 271
Bolsheviks, 271
Brass, 276, 281
Brazen altar, 143
Buddhists, 32

Calvary, 73, 77, 78, 111, 142, 145, 147, 158, 218
Carl Drexler, 203
Christian, 3, 9, 14, 18, 20, 21, 32, 50, 51, 53, 54, 55, 58, 59, 61, 75, 76, 127, 135, 144, 148, 150, 168, 173, 174, 221, 230, 231, 252, 253, 254, 255, 259, 262, 264, 265, 266, 268, 269, 280, 281, 283
Church, 11, 13, 17, 18, 30, 38, 56, 61, 62, 63, 86, 107, 122, 132, 144, 152, 155, 164, 172, 173, 177, 186, 198, 201, 207, 208, 209, 220, 222, 229, 231, 235, 236, 249, 251, 252, 253, 254, 255, 256, 257, 258, 260, 261, 262, 263, 266, 267, 268, 277, 282, 293
Commandments, 16, 160
Conditional, 121, 122
Cromwell, 49
Crusades, 56, 263
CUFI, 55, 63
Czarist, 270, 272
Dachau, 41, 42
Daniel Webster, 67
Davidic covenant, 118
Death camps, 42
Deborah Lipstadt, 43, 275
Deuteronomy, 74, 95, 109, 123, 130, 179, 198, 199, 207, 217
Diana Castro, 57
Dr. Walvoord, 118
Elijah complex, 170, 213
Esau, 79, 80, 81, 82, 177, 178, 179, 180
EUMC, 264
Evil, 129, 169
Exodus, 15, 27, 90, 91, 92, 93, 94,

INDEX OF WORDS AND PHRASES

95, 97, 98, 99, 101, 102, 105, 106, 107, 108, 113, 115, 122, 123, 124, 127, 148, 149, 151, 152, 153, 155, 156, 161, 162, 181, 239, 264, 276, 280
Fatah, 23
Fulfill, 138
Furthermore, thanks to Dr. and Mrs. Williams for their tireless work to complete these pages and turn them into a book. May God bless them for their Godly counsel., 3
Gainsaying, 208
Gods, 102, 277
Gold, 2
Gospel, 3, 58, 61, 62, 65, 155, 173, 200, 203, 204, 205, 206, 207, 208, 216, 220, 222, 223, 224, 228, 229, 231, 234, 241, 243, 244, 253, 265, 266, 280, 283
Grace, 12, 125, 215
Great Commission, 61, 227, 266
Hadrian, 167
Hamas Charter, 24, 25, 26, 31, 271, 273, 275
Harry Elmer Barnes, 39
Hebrew, 3, 15, 34, 59, 71, 75, 84, 88, 91, 92, 93, 100, 108, 122, 123, 142, 169, 191, 199, 206, 217, 252, 267
Hell, 30
Henry Ford, 272
Henry Rousso, 33
Hezbollah, 23, 46
Hindus, 32
Hitler, 30, 31, 33, 37, 39, 41, 45, 268, 269, 273
Holocaust, 27, 31, 32, 33, 34, 35, 36, 40, 42, 43, 44, 45, 54, 56,

264, 266, 275, 276, 280, 283
Holocaust Deniers, 31, 275
Honor, 54
Hosea, 22, 186, 187, 237, 258, 259
Isaac, 68, 69, 72, 76, 77, 78, 79, 80, 87, 88, 89, 92, 118, 175, 176, 177, 178, 179, 241, 280
Islam, 9, 14, 18, 19, 22, 23, 44, 46, 55, 214
Ismael, 72, 76, 178, 179
Israelites, 91, 92, 95, 96, 97, 100, 103, 105, 106, 107, 109, 110, 111, 112, 113, 114, 115, 122, 125, 127, 129, 130, 139, 145, 146, 147, 159, 160, 162, 163, 165, 170, 175, 176, 185, 190, 197, 198, 216, 220, 223, 224, 235, 239, 240
Jack Van Impe, 57
Jacob, 68, 69, 79, 80, 81, 82, 83, 84, 86, 87, 89, 90, 91, 92, 124, 128, 175, 176, 177, 178, 179, 180, 211, 234, 236, 241
Jerusalem, 12, 21, 22, 25, 27, 52, 53, 55, 61, 66, 78, 108, 158, 165, 166, 172, 191, 221, 236, 239, 251, 257
Jewish Lobby, 31
Joe Biden, 47, 48, 276
John Hagee, 54, 56, 57, 58, 59, 63, 282
Joseph, 68, 69, 81, 83, 84, 85, 86, 87, 90, 105, 179, 272
Kemalist, 46
King James Bible, 2, 22, 68, 74, 206, 277

INDEX OF WORDS AND PHRASES

Kotel, 55
Laban, 80, 81
Leah, 80, 81, 89
Locusts, 102
Martin Luther, 30, 251, 267, 269
Maurice Joly, 270
Mercy, 144, 151, 156, 158, 161, 162, 175, 181, 242
Messiah, 15, 17, 23, 29, 60, 66, 76, 77, 84, 88, 89, 133, 163, 164, 169, 176, 177, 193, 204, 205, 217, 218, 220, 229, 233, 236, 238, 240, 241, 243, 251, 257, 259, 283
Middle Easterners, 32
Midian, 92, 93
Mohammed, 9, 14, 18, 46, 178
Mosaic covenant, 63, 122
Moses, 12, 16, 59, 91, 92, 93, 94, 95, 96, 97, 98, 99, 101, 105, 106, 108, 115, 117, 124, 125, 127, 131, 132, 136, 137, 139, 146, 155, 160, 162, 175, 180, 184, 185, 191, 196, 197, 198, 200, 205, 207, 266
Muslims, 9, 14, 18, 32, 45
Nazi, 33, 34, 35, 36, 37, 38, 39, 40, 41, 42, 45, 52, 257, 276
Nebuchadnezzar, 30
Nile, 85, 98, 273
Noahic, 123
Osiris, 98, 102
Palestinian, 17, 23, 24, 25, 26, 53, 56
Parker Yockey, 37
Passover, 104, 106, 110, 111, 112, 113, 218, 264, 283
Paul, 42, 57, 58, 60, 63, 111, 129, 130, 131, 139,

164, 168, 169, 171, 172, 173, 174, 175, 176, 177, 180, 181, 182, 183, 185, 188, 190, 191, 192, 193, 194, 195, 196, 200, 201, 203, 204, 205, 206, 207, 208, 209, 211, 212, 214, 215, 216, 217, 218, 219, 222, 223, 224, 226, 227, 229, 231, 232, 233, 234, 237, 241, 242, 244, 245, 246, 256, 258, 259, 260, 274, 279, 281

Pentateuch, 67, 281

Pentecost, 11, 118, 172, 220, 235, 255, 258, 283

Pharaoh, 11, 30, 85, 86, 91, 93, 95, 97, 98, 99, 100, 101, 102, 103, 104, 105, 108, 114, 116, 180, 182, 184, 216

Phinehas, 195

Plague, 98

Plains Baptist Challenger, 57, 282

PLO, 23

Pompey, 166

Positive Confession, 58

Presbyterian Church, 61

Preterism, 254, 281

Promised land, 111

Racism, 278

Rebekah, 78, 79, 80, 89

Red Sea, 30, 115, 116, 117

Replacement theology, 252, 262

Replacement Theology, 18, 30, 249, 256, 277, 282, 283

Rome, 166, 172, 194, 230, 231, 234, 242, 263

INDEX OF WORDS AND PHRASES

Sarah, 69, 71, 72, 75, 76, 79, 89, 177, 178
Serge Nilus, 271
Seventy weeks, 240
Sharia Law, 19, 24, 25
Shekinah, 140, 175, 221
Shiloh, 88
Shylock, 47, 48, 49, 50, 51, 52, 276
Sinai, 16, 95, 115, 124, 131, 140, 176, 194, 239
Sodom and Gomorrah, 189
Spanish Inquisition, 56
Succoth, 115
Supersessionism, 18, 249, 251, 253, 277, 283
Temple Mount, 25
Terah, 69, 118
The law, 16, 125, 126, 130, 131, 135, 138, 139, 176, 197
The Protocols of Zion, 282

The tabernacle, 139, 142, 144
The veil, 144, 156, 157, 158
Theodicy, 167, 168
Trajan, 166
Tribulation, 9, 10, 11, 17, 18, 23, 71, 170, 188, 217, 236, 237, 238, 239, 240, 254, 260, 261
Unconditional, 121, 123, 124
Venice, 48, 49, 51, 52
Vespasian, 165
Waqf, 24, 25
Weimar Republic, 42
West Bank, 52
Wilderness, 141, 175
William Shakespeare, 48
Willis A. Carto, 36, 275
World War II, 31, 33, 34, 36, 40, 41, 43
Yasser Arafat, 53
Zeal, 195

Zion, 27, 210, 239, 270, 271, 273, 280

ABOUT THE AUTHOR

Dr. Charles Kriessman has been saved since the Lord called him on September 12, 1983. He attends The Bible for Today Church in Collingswood, New Jersey, via Internet Streaming, since 2004. Pastor D.A. Waite, Th.D., Ph.D. is the Pastor of BFT.

Charles was born in Washington, D.C. sixty-four years ago. He has studied the subject of Bible Versions since 1985. He has written a book on the subject entitled, "Modern Version Failures."

He has attended Gustavus Adolphus College in St. Peter, Minnesota; Orange Coast College in Costa Mesa, California; and Macedonia Baptist College in Midland, North Carolina. Dr. Kriessman currently holds a Masters and Doctorate degrees in Biblical Studies from G.C.B.I. in Ft. Walton Beach, Florida.